T0300872

UNIVERSITY OF CAMBRIDGE
DEPARTMENT OF APPLIED ECONOMICS

MONOGRAPHS

2

SOCIAL ACCOUNTS
AND THE
BUSINESS ENTERPRISE SECTOR
OF THE
NATIONAL ECONOMY

UNIVERSITY OF CAMBRIDGE
DEPARTMENT OF APPLIED ECONOMICS

MONOGRAPHS

This series consists of investigations conducted by members of the Department's staff and others working in direct collaboration with the Department.

The Department of Applied Economics assumes no responsibility for the views expressed in the Monographs published under its auspices.

1. The Measurement of Production Movements
By C. F. CARTER, W. B. REDDAWAY, AND RICHARD STONE

2. Social Accounts of the Business Enterprise Sector
of the National Economy
By F. SEWELL BRAY

SOCIAL ACCOUNTS

AND THE

BUSINESS ENTERPRISE SECTOR

OF THE

NATIONAL ECONOMY

BY

F. SEWELL BRAY

SENIOR NUFFIELD RESEARCH FELLOW
DEPARTMENT OF APPLIED ECONOMICS
CAMBRIDGE

CAMBRIDGE
AT THE UNIVERSITY PRESS
1949

CAMBRIDGE UNIVERSITY PRESS
Cambridge, New York, Melbourne, Madrid, Cape Town,
Singapore, São Paulo, Delhi, Mexico City

Cambridge University Press
The Edinburgh Building, Cambridge CB2 8RU, UK

Published in the United States of America by Cambridge University Press, New York

www.cambridge.org
Information on this title: www.cambridge.org/9781107665125

First published 1949
Re-issued 2013

A catalogue record for this publication is available from the British Library

ISBN 978-1-107-66512-5 Paperback

CONTENTS

PREFACE

A big advance in national income research was made in this country in 1937 when in his book *National Income and Outlay* Colin Clark brought together figures not only of total income and its components but also of consumption, saving, capital (or asset) formation, public authority income and outlay and transactions with the rest of the world. Most of what is interesting in this branch of economics is derived precisely from tracing the relationships between such magnitudes as these, and certainly from the practical point of view of the user of such calculations engaged in the task of guiding and interpreting economic policy, little can be done with isolated series of one or other element in the picture. This at least was the point of view adopted by J. E. Meade and myself when we worked together on these problems in the early stages of the war and the rapid development of social (or national) accounting in the statistical work of many governments bears witness to the soundness of this view.

At first the problems of ensuring consistency in the treatment of transactions was tackled in terms of national aggregates, like the national income and expenditure, or of the consolidated transactions of large sectors such as 'persons'. It came to be realised that conceptually the basic material for such studies is the set of ideal entries in a highly complex accounting system in which every accounting entity is represented. In these terms, the problem becomes—how to set up such an accounting system so as to provide the information sought by the economist and how to combine or consolidate the accounts in the system so as to yield meaningful and consistent aggregates.

I endeavoured to provide some sort of solution to these problems in a memorandum entitled *Definition and Measurement of the National Income and Related Totals*, which was discussed by the Sub-Committee on National Income Statistics of the League of Nations Committee of Statistical Experts at their meeting in Princeton, N.J., at the end of 1945 and subsequently appeared as an appendix to the Sub-Committee's report *Measurement of National Income and the Construction of Social Accounts* (1947). This report and the memorandum appended to it have subsequently been used as a general framework for the investigations of the Statistical Office of the United Nations embodied in *National Income Statistics 1938–1947* (1948), prepared under the direction of J. B. D. Derksen.

When the stage of discussing problems of definition and measurement in accounting terms had been reached, the next task was to make sure that the accounting was sound from a professional accounting point of view. By 'sound' I do not mean that the economists' accounting systems should adopt existing accounting conventions on every point. I mean rather that the accounting systems should be drawn up with a proper knowledge of the many complicated transactions that actually take place in an economy, and that they should be designed in detail with due regard to the character and limitations of business records. Such considerations as these are important from a conceptual point of view, but appropriate design takes on an added importance if the necessary information is to be collected on the basis of samples of different types of account. Sampling procedure of this kind, given the possibilities of greatly improved economic and statistical design in this field of investigation which it holds out, cannot be contemplated however until a detailed study has been made of the practical difficulties involved. The present volume, which deals only with business enterprises, is the first fruits of such an enquiry.

The manuscript for this monograph was completed in the early summer of 1947. During the preceding year, and for some time after, Mr Bray and I were members of a joint sub-committee of accountants and economists brought together by the Institute of Chartered Accountants and the National Institute of Economic and Social Research. The terms of reference of the sub-committee were to report on terms and concepts in common use by accountants and economists. Mr Bray and I would like to record the mental stimulus we received from our colleagues on this sub-committee without of course committing the sub-committee or either of the convening organisations to any of the views that appear in this study.

J. R. N. S.

CAMBRIDGE
May 1949

I

THE DOUBLE-ENTRY SYSTEM AND ITS PURPOSE

The basis of the double-entry system of social accounts for the business enterprise sector of the national economy which is here put forward, is to be found in 'A Working System of Social Accounting', a study which forms part of Mr Richard Stone's memorandum on the subject of 'Definition and Measurement of the National Income and Related Totals'. This memorandum was included as the appendix to the Report of the Sub-Committee on National Income Statistics of the League of Nations Committee of Statistical Experts.

The originating structure of accounts is set out in the second section of this book, and it will be clear to both accountants and business men that it reveals a grasp of double-entry account keeping principles. Accordingly, it should not prove a difficult matter to reset this originating structure in a form reasonably consistent with and acceptable to current accounting practice.

At this point it is worth while recalling some comments of Mr G. O. May, a leading American accounting authority. Writing on the uses of accounts with particular reference to concepts of income he made it clear that

...double-entry accounting supplies a check which is invaluable. Industrial experience has repeatedly demonstrated the dangers inherent in computations of costs or profits which are not so tied in with the financial accounts as to insure that all costs have been allocated in one way or another. Today, such integration is recognised as indispensable to the establishment of reliable factual bases for policies and actions.

There he reveals the statistical check which double-entry financial accounting documents do portray. Each recorded originating transaction must have its counterpart somewhere in this system, only thus do we see the mutual interdependence of otherwise economically distinct transactions.

Mr G. O. May goes on to say that

The importance of this point and its wide applicability are apparent to anyone who has examined with care the purely statistical information in regard to the so-called national income and savings that has been officially disseminated, including that presented by distinguished economists in testimony before the Temporary National Economic Committee or in monographs published under the auspices of that body. If such material had always been the product of a rigorous system of double-entry accounting, many fallacies and unwarranted conclusions would have been avoided.

He quotes Professor Schumpeter as speaking of double-entry account keeping as the 'towering monument' of a practice which 'turns the unit of money into a tool of rational cost-profit calculations'. Mr G. O. May adds the comments that: 'It is to be feared that most economists and statisticians regard double-entry bookkeeping as just that—a monument to be admired from afar, rather than a technique to be acquired. They are less attracted by its humbler virtues than by the dangerous charms of extrapolation.'[1] These are comments which in the light of the memorandum we have mentioned cannot now be maintained in any sense intended by their author, but rather it may perhaps be wondered that no trained accountant ever seems to have consciously sought a social accounting approach to national income studies.

The present work is a utilitarian attempt to adapt and reset the originating accounts, in that sector of the national economy which is concerned with business enterprises, into a form in which it is hoped it will be readily and easily assimilated both by accountants and economists. Later, it is intended to rearrange the form of accounts in the other sectors in much the same way. Not all accountants may agree with the technical treatment of some of the items as now placed in the revised system and certainly economists may find much which, because it is related to so-called accounting principles and conventions, may seem to conflict with the more cherished theoretical notions of their subject. Nevertheless, it is put forward as a practical effort to reconcile the technique of the trained accountant with the conceptions of the economist, and as such it must stand or fall as individual judgment may determine. Much will have been accomplished if financial accounting statements in their more commonly accepted forms of balance-sheet and profit-and-loss account are recognised as statistical documents in the field of applied economics. Nevertheless, the potentialities of financial accounting documents can only be fully realised if they adhere to the primary detail suggested by the aggregated forms put forward in Sections VII and IX of this book. The ordinary run of *published* accounts so far available to the economic investigator are not sufficiently complete to serve these ends; they cover some parts of the recommended system, but not others. The necessities of the times may impose other developments in regard to the collection of accounting information, but be that as it may, it would be of great assistance if published accounts could be made more informative, although it should not be overlooked that the recommendations of the Cohen Committee on Company Law Amendment have taken the matter a stage further in this direction. Whatever practical difficulties may suggest themselves to business managements on the score of expediency, there is no doubt that one very real disadvantage to economists is the absence of reasonably detailed operating accounts. Perhaps it might be mentioned that in America this is far less a problem since there it seems to be thought a matter of some consequence to publish fairly full operating accounts.

Not the least of the problems associated with this work has been

[1] From George O. May, *Financial Accounting*, pp. 14, 15 (New York, 1943). By permission of The Macmillan Company (Publishers).

concerned with terminology. It has not proved an easy matter to suggest expressions which convey the same ideas to both economists and accountants. It is true that much of the groundwork was made plain in the originating structure of accounts particularly in regard to the use of that elusive word 'investment', but we were still left with the expressions 'capital formation', 'reserve account' and such like items which carried with them implications peculiar to the technique of accountancy not altogether intended in their original social accounting presentation. Moreover, the convention of imputation sounds an unfamiliar note to those accountants who are not versed in national income studies. Clearly, there is a need for some common terminology which will convey like ideas to both economists and accountants, and in Section VIII of this book we have sought to make a start in this direction side by side with the attempt to explain some of the major items as now set in the revised system of accounts. At Section x we have added a glossary of terms. In accounting parlance capital and asset are distinct terms in the sense that the one signifies the contribution of money which financed the acquisition of the other. In some measure they are indeed reciprocal, but accountants recognising their intimate concern with proprietorship interests have consistently identified the money contributions to, and money savings of an enterprise, for the very good reason that the first cause of their financial accounting documents has been the disclosure of ability to preserve money capital, and to extend the ownership equity of redemption in money terms (chiefly by means of retained profits—reserve or surplus as it is known in the technical language of accountants). Thus it is thought that a change of expression such as 'asset formation', 'inventory formation' and the like, will at least reveal to accountants some of the questions to which economists are urgently seeking answers in their efforts to lay bare the real elements which make for the collective material well-being of society.

It is probably not altogether surprising that accountants have allowed the money end of things to exert a firm grip over their minds. They have been tempted into regarding the monetary expression of real things as a matter of first importance—and most of their conventions are set to this end. Economists view their problems the other way round. Thus, it falls to accountants to recognise their money figures as a kind of shorthand for the expression of real things particularly when it comes to questions which concern the operating and asset accounts of business enterprises. Once this *is* recognised it will be seen that there is nothing so very mysterious about social accounts or about economic conceptions of the national income, the national capital, savings, asset formation, inventory formation and so on.

The working system of social accounts as built up in the originating structure is designed to facilitate the abstraction of certain highly significant national aggregates, e.g. the national income. As a matter of accounting convenience the interconnecting activities of the national economy involving money flows and related book-keeping transactions are first classified into certain broad sectors. Thus, there is a sector for productive enterprises, for financial intermediaries, for insurance and social security agencies, for final consumers and for the transactions with the rest of the world. A set of accounts is then built up for each sector to display the transactions which have taken place within that sector during a given accounting period. Each entry in these accounts represents an economically distinct category of transactions which is nevertheless related to its counterpart elsewhere in the system; this reciprocal entry may reside either in the accounts of the same or some other sector. The accounts which are here put forward in respect of the business enterprise sector are of a general overall nature, but it will be appreciated that a later development may require a breaking down to accord with a classification which will emphasise particular industrial activities, e.g. agriculture, mining, manufacturing of different kinds, transport, merchanting, and the like.[1] Or again, another classification may be designed on geographical lines according to the type of information sought by the economic investigator.

The national income and other similar aggregates are obtained from the complete system of social accounts particular to any one national economy by a process of selecting and bringing together a number of the constituent entries in the accounts. Thus, the national income is calculated by combining the income shares of the factors of production in the forms of wages and salaries, interest, operating surpluses and net dividends received from the rest of the world. Other equivalent and related totals may be calculated to arrive at the net national product at factor cost and the net national expenditure at factor cost. Again, a statement of the national income in terms of income payments may be built up from the same accounting source together with a clear indication of the relation between national income and gross national product, with a breakdown of the gross national product in terms of an expenditure classification. The same process may be used to throw up the constituent figures making up total saving together with the use of this saving in net asset formation by enterprises of all kinds, persons and public collective providers, and to show the balancing total for net lending to the rest of the world. Moreover, the receivables and payables of public authorities may be conveniently brought together in the form of a consolidated account of social security funds and public collective providers. Once more it should not be overlooked that a complete adoption of accounting technique to the point of the preparation of an aggregated national balance sheet will give a reasonably clear indication of the make-up of the national capital, and in Section IX of this book the reader will find that a first start has been made in this direction with a *pro forma* balance sheet, in simple outline, worked out on the basis of a complete aggregation of individual enterprise balance sheets. This balance sheet deals with the business enterprise sector only, but clearly

[1] At least a broad general classification between capital and consumption goods industries seems desirable.

it should not be impossible to devise similar balance-sheet forms for the other sectors, and then to bring these balance sheets together in the shape of one such document for the whole national economy. Thus, it is plain that a social accounting set up on the lines which have been indicated should promote a clearer understanding of the elemental groups of transactions entering into the calculation of significant national aggregates, and of their interdependence on one another.[1]

The technique of private accounting is very largely wedded to record and statement in terms of historical costs and historical revenues. Social accounting on the other hand may require a development of this technique in terms of either a current money measure or a standardised money measure of real things, particularly when it comes to such questions as national capital aggregates, asset and inventory formations and so on. Suggestions for the adaptation of private accounting statements to meet this development will be found in Section VIII of this work where explanations are given of the major items in the revised double-entry system now put forward. Nevertheless, social accounting does very largely resolve itself into a matter of the aggregation of private accounting statements, particularly in relation to the business enterprise sector of the national economy. The essential feature of this process of aggregation is the portrayal of income generation over a stated interval of time, and in this context it seems better to emphasise the expression aggregation rather than promote the use of a term like consolidation, since the latter has rather special technical implications for accountants which arise out of its use in connection with the presentation of accounting statements which will reflect the position and earnings of a holding company and its subsidiary companies, as a business unit from the standpoint of the shareholding proprietors of the holding company. Yet the mechanics of aggregation are not unlike the mechanics of consolidation, more particularly when we come to consider the pressing need for uniformity. Yet nothing seems to provoke such differences of opinion among accountants as this question of uniformity in the statement and presentation of accounts. So we have Mr G. O. May saying that

the demand for uniformity in financial accounting is as natural as the demand for certainty—and as incapable of being met. Accounts are historical records, but they cannot rise higher in the scale of certainty than the knowledge which they reflect. Nor is it always possible when uniformity is sought to say whether the resemblances or the differences between transactions are the more significant.

[1] It is contemplated that all significant national aggregates will be put into such a form as to allow of one complete set of accounts for the whole economy. In simple outline terms the profit-and-loss account will take the form

$$\text{National income} - \text{consumption} = \text{saving.}$$

The resting account will exhibit the identity

$$\text{Saving} = \text{net lending} + \text{net asset formation,}$$

while the national balance sheet will illustrate the formula

$$\text{National capital} = \text{assets} - \text{liabilities.}$$

Yet he does concede that 'uniformity in the treatment of routine transactions is undoubtedly practicable and of great value for a number of administrative purposes'.[1] It is true that private financial accounts are required for all kinds of purposes peculiar to the individual business units for the benefit of which they are prepared, but when we come to aggregation in the service of the calculation of national aggregates there is only one primary purpose involved and quite clearly aggregated totals are going to mean nothing at all unless the constituent items have been stated and classified on a like basis. Whatever individual firms may require to serve their own ends it is apparent that if social accounting is to become a practical matter then there must be uniformity in the statement of primary data even though for some of them this may require the preparation of a special form of accounts. There have been some accountants who have been quick to recognise the need for uniform accounting practices when it comes to the point of consolidating company accounts. Thus Mr T. B. Robson has said quite firmly that

the preparation of consolidated accounts is greatly assisted by the adherence of all companies in the group to a uniform classification of accounting items and a standard accounting practice. The issue to all concerned of accounting instructions designed to secure conformity with this practice not only as between companies but also as between one financial period and another is of the greatest value. Many groups prepare monthly accounts on a con-solidated basis and the importance of having a clearly prescribed routine in such cases will be readily apparent.[2]

Here we have the lesser case for uniformity and it does not seem a far step to see its projection as a necessity in the field of social accounting.

As is well known, private accounts are made up at different dates, and aggregation as the matter stands is bound to result in some distortion, unless some attempt is made at uniformity in the selection of a time period which is common to all accounting units entering into the social accounting system. The natural period which should commend itself to accountants no less than economists is the fiscal year ending on 5 April, since it would near enough conform to the accounting periods of public authorities and would avoid much of the mechanics of taxation liability apportionment. No doubt many will feel that this is an ideal which will provoke too many practical difficulties in the preparation of uniform primary financial data by individual enterprises, on the grounds that such information is too intimately bound up with the periodical financial accounting statements of such undertakings. Perhaps then, as a first start we might follow a practice of the Inland Revenue, aggregating accounts whose year-end dates fall within the selected period. Or, again, we might follow the somewhat rough-and-ready procedure of a time apportionment. Perhaps it might not be too unwarrantable even

---

[1] From George O. May, *Financial Accounting*, p. 249 (New York, 1943). By permission of The Macmillan Company (Publishers).

[2] *Holding Companies and their Subsidiaries: Consolidated Accounts, Principles and Procedure*, by T. B. Robson, p. 25 (London: Gee and Company (Publishers), Limited, 1946).

to suggest the provision of quarterly statements, for this would present far less difficulties to the statistical aggregator in his attempt to set the social accounting picture over a given interval of time. But whatever procedure is followed we must ultimately look forward to uniformity if unreal distortion is to be avoided, although we should not forget that even approximations may yield interesting figures when it is mainly comparisons that are sought.

As we have said, this book has been planned on the basis of the working system of social accounting prepared by Mr Richard Stone, and his originating structure of accounts is set out in Section II. At Section III there are a series of originating reconciliations designed to show the reciprocal nature of the constituent entries in the originating structure; accountants will look upon these reconciliations as a series of journal entries. Section IV contains the primary reconciliations which are intended to show the opening and closing adjustments for debtors and creditors, unexpired payments, accrued expenses and such-like items, to give the receivables and payables of the revised double-entry system. For the sake of comprehension and to make reference easy, the receivables and payables of the new system have been made more or less equivalent to the items in the originating system. This should enable most items in the new system to be picked up in the originating system.

We should add that all this is not to suggest that the originating structure was intended to be limited to receipts and payments. It plainly recognised the implications associated with receivables and payables by providing a write-off for bad debts in the operating account of business enterprises. Economists *do* think in terms of receivables and payables even though they may sometimes call them receipts and payments, and there is no real difference of opinion between accountants and economists on this point. The real problem raised by the accrual method of accounting was abstracted away in the originating system in order to simplify the presentation, but in the revised system now put forward the attempt has been made to show the effect of debtor-creditor adjustments.

To those accustomed to looking at national income and expenditure statements as usually set out in the past it may seem confusing that in the revised system of accounts payables have been set on the left-hand side and receivables on the right-hand side, although to the accountant it will seem the more natural treatment. The distinction arises out of the technical setting of a cash account in terms of actual receipts and actual payments. A cash account in accountancy technique is one of prime entry. When money is received it is entered on the left-hand side of this account where it becomes an originating transaction. To preserve the system of double-entry a reciprocal destination entry is then made to the right-hand side of a classified ledger account. This account is more commonly one of secondary entry and its main purposes, for example in the case of an operating revenue, is to bring together like receipts, to show opening and closing adjustments for debtors, and to so arrive at a total for the classified *receivables* of the relevant accounting period. Since these receivables have been ascertained through the medium of a secondary account they appear on the right-hand side of any summary of ledger balances in contradistinction to a cash receipt which appears on the left-hand side of a cash account. In most cases to find an item on the right-hand side of a summarised operating account is to infer that it is a receivable rather than a receipt. In the same way and for much the same reasons an item on the left-hand side is usually a payable. A glance at a published company profit and loss account prepared in any detail will confirm this, since the expense items will show on the left-hand side and the revenue items on the right-hand side.

Section v of this book contains statements setting out the so-called opening and closing circulating capital funds. These statements, as their name implies, are very largely made up of the circulating capital items at the opening and closing accounting dates. Accountants will probably prefer to regard them as detailed statements of current assets and current liabilities. Thus, they contain the details of debtors and creditors, unexpired payments, accrued revenues and accrued expenses, the inventory figures, proposed dividends and so on. It will be seen that they find their places in the aggregated resting account (where they are analysed in terms of inventories, debtors and creditors, and bank and cash balances), and in the sector balance sheets, more particularly that balance sheet which is limited to the entries of the period.

In Section vi of this work will be found a summarised schedule of balances showing the group make-up of each item, and which is here called the balancing statement. Accountants will be more familiar with the title of trial balance. The purpose of this statement is to show by the technical accounting apparatus of the trial balance that all the group items entering into the system of accounts are in balance. Thus the total debit entries are shown to be equivalent to the total credit entries, and the self balancing nature of the system is established.

The revised system of accounts, adjusted to conform with accounting conceptions of the statement of accounts, is set out in Section ix, and it will be noticed that it follows much the same lines as the originating structure. It begins with an aggregated profit-and-loss account of business enterprises subdivided into two sections, the one described as operating and the other as non-operating. The operating section is concerned with all those items which go into the measurement of the operating surplus or profit of business enterprises. In the non-operating section will be found items of investment and imputed incomes, net realised capital gains available for application as income, insurance claims for consequential losses, direct taxes, and non-operating expenses.

Where enterprises are engaged in subsidiary economic activities, e.g. the letting of properties, these should be the subject of separate operating accounts, the resulting surpluses on these accounts being thereafter transferred to the account for income from sources external to the main operations. It will be realised that it is the process of generating income which we are concerned to emphasise in the operating accounts. Only quite recently one accountant has reminded us that

the distinction between the income which is created by a corporation or enterprise and that of which it is merely the transferee is important, but is inadequately recognised in most discussions of accounting principles and procedures. Realization is regarded as a crucial test in accounting; but a realization which represents the culmination of a process of creating income has an altogether different significance from that of a realization which is merely a transfer to a beneficiary of income already created by the transferor. A useful advance in corporate and financial practice would be effected if the distinction between 'income from operations' and 'transfer income' should become more universally emphasized.[1]

We might add that this is indeed one of the main distinctions sought by the division of the profit-and-loss account into operating and non-operating sections. As accountants would expect, the profit-and-loss account is followed by an aggregated appropriation account which is intended to portray the available income from all sources applicable to the relevant accounting period, that part of it which is distributed by way of dividends and withdrawals and that part of it which is reserved as savings retained in the enterprises.

It will be noticed that the originating capital and reserve accounts have now been dovetailed into one account which has been renamed the resting account. This has been done to bring this part of the system more nearly into line with the self-balancing conceptions of accounting technique. On the one side will be found the capital funds made available during the period, in the accounting sense of that expression, while on the other side is shown the application of those funds in asset formation and investment acquisitions. It should be explained that the term 'resting' for this account is used in the sense that it does not enter into the main profit-and-loss account.[2] A special feature of this account in the revised system is the place to be found for the increase or decrease in circulating capital resources (analysed in terms of inventories, debtors and creditors, and bank and cash balances) as between the start and end of the accounting period. An increase in these resources constitutes an addition to capital funds while a decrease represents an application of capital funds otherwise acquired.

In Section IX of this work the adaptation of the double-entry accounting technique to the originating structure of accounts is carried to its ultimate conclusion by the provision of sector balance sheets. Since the originating entries were limited to an accounting period the first of these business enterprise balance sheets perforce has been designed on these

---

[1] From George O. May, *Financial Accounting*, p. 25 (New York, 1943). By permission of The Macmillan Company (Publishers).

[2] Cf. the references to resting accounts in Dr H. W. Singer's *Standardized Accountancy in Germany*, pp. 19 and 67 (National Institute of Economic and Social Research, Occasional Paper, v; Cambridge: University Press, 1943).

lines. It follows the commonly accepted accounting form represented by the equation

$$\text{Assets} - \text{Liabilities} = \text{Capital} + \text{Surplus},$$

and in this context it should be remarked that borrowed money is treated on the footing of a liability and thereby distinguished from contributed capital. In general terms a clear distinction is made on the left-hand side of this balance sheet in regard to all forms of borrowing including contributed capital, the fund for depreciation and replacement, current and deferred liabilities. On the right-hand side of this balance sheet the main groupings relate to gross fixed asset formation, investments in securities, current assets and deferred charges. It should be explained that the excess of current assets over current liabilities constitutes a measure of what economists would ordinarily regard as circulating capital and accountants as working capital. We might add that current assets is used in the sense of those assets which 'are held for realisation in the ordinary course of business'.[1] The reader will recognise that when the balance sheets for each sector of the economy finally come to be amalgamated the debtors and creditors as between the different sectors will cancel out.

A second and *pro forma* balance sheet has been drafted in simple outline on the basis of a complete aggregation of individual enterprise balance sheets, and its relevance to the ultimate calculation of an aggregate for national capital will not pass unnoticed. In general it has been put together in terms of historical costs so far as concerns the definite figures, with the exception of the asset replacement provision carried into the depreciation fund. It will also be noticed that under the heading of fixed asset formation an estimated replacement valuation adjustment has been added as an inset to the customary original cost figures, in order to give the replacement value of the fixed assets carried. We recognise the complications associated with the conception of replacement[2] value, complications to which we have ourselves drawn attention in Section VIII of this book. Nevertheless, whether the attempt be made on a physical replacement basis or by reference to a price index either general or specific as applied to original costs (and for ourselves we feel that specific indices should be resorted to if this method is followed), it is clear that some *current* monetary measure must be applied to this grouping if money aggregates of national capital are to be given any real meaning.

The grouping for investments has been so sorted out as to throw up the par equivalents, an essential pivotal series when it comes to the amalgamation of all the sector balance sheets. For the benefit of accountants perhaps it should be explained that conceptions such as pre-acquisition profits, while they are of material relevance in the

---

[1] *Recommendations on Accounting Principles of the Institute of Chartered Accountants in England and Wales*, p. 22 (Gee and Company (Publishers), Limited).

[2] Or current cost.

display of the consolidated results of groups of companies, have little or no point when it becomes a matter of the aggregation of all enterprise accounts within the social structure, since in the latter connection the main intent is to lay bare the real aggregated net assets of the national economy. Accountants will recognise that the expression 'other items' as brought in under the heading of deferred charges is intended to cover the familiar company suspense debits in respect of preliminary, formation, issue expenses and the like.

We would close with the comment that although we have consistently raised the issue of so-called social accounts, no attempt has been made in any of the accounting presentations put forward here to carry in any sort of conventions to deal with social costs and social benefits. Later, we may hope to set about this task, but for the moment the expression social accounting is only used in contradistinction to private accounting. In the ordinary course of the day-to-day affairs of the working of the national economy private accounting as defined in this context is oriented to the safeguarding of proprietorship interests, and its aggregation as we set it forth is intended to carry the *same* accounting process yet one stage further by bringing it on to the level of the standpoint of society as a whole. Much of the discussion on the maintenance of capital intact centres in this development. As we have hinted, there is still much more to be done, but for the present such a system as we have advocated should ultimately make for greater accuracy in calculation and better comprehension of the interrelatedness of the national aggregates to which we have repeatedly referred.

II

THE ORIGINATING STRUCTURE
OF ACCOUNTS

SECTOR I. PRODUCTIVE ENTERPRISES
Business Enterprises

(1) Operating account   (3) Capital account
(2) Appropriation account   (4) Reserve account

Persons (house-ownership)

(5) Operating account

SECTOR II. FINANCIAL INTERMEDIARIES
Banking System

(6) Operating account   (8) Capital and reserve account
(7) Appropriation account

Other Financial Intermediaries

(9) Operating account   (11) Capital and reserve account
(10) Appropriation account

SECTOR III. INSURANCE AND SOCIAL SECURITY AGENCIES
Insurance Companies and Societies

(12) Revenue accounts: (13) Operating account
  (a) Enterprises, etc.   (14) Appropriation account
  (b) Final consumers   (15) Capital and reserve account
  (c) Rest of the world

Private Pension Funds

(16) Revenue account   (17) Capital and reserve account

Social Security Funds

(18) Revenue account   (19) Capital and reserve account

SECTOR IV. FINAL CONSUMERS
Persons

(20) Revenue account   (21) Capital and reserve account

Public Collective Providers

(22) Revenue account   (23) Capital and reserve account

SECTOR V. REST OF THE WORLD
All Economic Entities

(24) Consolidated account

SECTOR I. BUSINESS ENTERPRISES

(1) OPERATING ACCOUNT

1. Sales proceeds	50,000	5. Payments to factors of production	
2. Subsidies	130	(a) Wages, salaries, etc.	3,975
3. Transfer from capital account in respect of unsold goods, work in progress and unused materials	70	(b) Interest	500
		6. Purchases of goods and services including bank and similar charges, actual and imputed	43,025
		7. Insurance premiums and imputed charges to policyholders	80
		8. Indirect taxes	270
		9. Contribution to social security funds	30
		10. Transfer to capital account in respect of inventories taken over	55
		11. Transfer to capital account in respect of depreciation and obsolescence	440
		12. Transfer to revenue account of persons in respect of bad debts	25
		13. Transfer to appropriation account of surplus	1,800
4. Total receipts	50,200	14. Total payments	50,200

(2) APPROPRIATION ACCOUNT

15. Transfer from operating account of surplus	1,800	24. Dividends and withdrawals	1,600
16. Interest	10	25. Direct taxes	300
17. Receipts in respect of deposits actual and imputed	95	26. Payments of contingency claims to employees and third parties (assumed to be handled by insurance rather than reserves)	15
18. Imputed receipts as policyholders	5	27. Transfer to capital account in respect of property insurance claims	35
19. Dividends	120		
20. Insurance claims	55		
21. Transfer from reserve in respect of excess provision for taxation	5	28. Transfer to reserve in respect of unpaid accruing tax liability	45
22. Transfer from reserve in respect of realised capital gains	15	29. Transfer to reserve of surplus	110
23. Total receipts	2,105	30. Total payments	2,105

(3) CAPITAL ACCOUNT

31. Transfer from operating account in respect of inventories taken over	55	36. Payments to factors of production	
		(a) Wages, salaries, etc.	135
32. Transfer from operating account in respect of depreciation and obsolescence	440	37. Purchases of goods and services	800
		38. Net purchases of existing equipment and other assets	15
33. Transfer from appropriation account in respect of property insurance claims	35	39. Transfer to operating account in respect of unsold goods, work in progress and unused materials	70
34. Transfer from reserve account	490		
35. Total receipts	1,020	40. Total payments	1,020

(4) RESERVE ACCOUNT

41. Transfer from appropriation account in respect of unpaid accruing tax liability	45	47. Transfer to appropriation account in respect of excess provision for taxation	5
42. Transfer from appropriation account of surplus	110	48. Transfer to appropriation account in respect of realised capital gains	15
43. Receipts from subscription to new issues, etc.	345	49. Transfer to capital account	490
44. Other new borrowing from		50. Net sums deposited with banks and given in return for notes and coin	40
(a) Banks	25		
(b) Other financial intermediaries	40	51. Subscriptions to new issues, etc.	5
45. Receipts from redemptions and repayments	15	52. Net purchases of existing securities	5
		53. Redemption and repayment of obligations	20
46. Total receipts	580	54. Total payments	580

Persons (house-ownership)

(5) OPERATING ACCOUNT

55. Gross rental received or imputed	500	57. Payments to factors of production	
		(a) Wages, salaries, etc.	70
		(b) Interest	20
		58. Purchases of goods and services	45
		59. Insurance premiums	30
		60. Indirect taxes	120
		61. Transfer to personal capital and reserve account in respect of depreciation and obsolescence	50
		62. Transfer to personal revenue account of surplus	165
56. Total receipts	500	63. Total payments	500

SECTOR II. FINANCIAL INTERMEDIARIES

Banking System

(6) OPERATING ACCOUNT

64. Charges to customers actual and imputed		66. Payments to factors of production	
(a) Actual		(a) Wages, salaries, etc.	95
(i) Business enterprises	5	67. Purchases of goods and services	45
(ii) Persons	20	68. Insurance premiums	5
(b) Imputed		69. Indirect taxes	5
(i) Business enterprises	25	70. Transfer to appropriation account of surplus	50
(ii) Persons	150		
65. Total receipts	200	71. Total payments	200

(7) Appropriation Account

72. Transfer from operating account of surplus	50	77. Payments to depositors actual and imputed	
73. Interest	200	(a) Actual	
74. Dividends	50	(i) Business enterprises	45
75. Insurance claims	...	(ii) Persons	30
		(b) Imputed	
		(i) Business enterprises	25
		(ii) Persons	150
		78. Dividends and withdrawals	35
		79. Direct taxes	10
		80. Transfer to capital and reserve of surplus	5
76. Total receipts	300	81. Total payments	300

(8) Capital and Reserve Account

82. Transfer from appropriation account of surplus	5	87. Net purchases of gold and silver bullion and coin	15
83. Net sums deposited and received in return for notes and coin	65	88. Net sums deposited and given in return for notes and coin	...
84. Receipts from subscriptions to new issues	5	89. Discounts and advances to	
		(a) Business enterprises	25
85. Receipts from redemptions and repayments	10	(b) Persons	5
		90. Subscriptions to new issues, etc.	35
		91. Net purchases of existing securities	5
		92. Redemptions and repayments of obligations	...
86. Total receipts	85	93. Total payments	85

Other Financial Intermediaries

(9) Operating Account

94. Charges to customers actual and imputed		96. Payments to factors of production	
(a) Actual		(a) Wages, salaries, etc.	120
(i) Business enterprises	15	97. Purchases of goods and services	30
(ii) Persons	135	98. Insurance premiums	10
(b) Imputed		99. Indirect taxes	5
(i) Business enterprises	5	100. Transfer to appropriation account of surplus	40
(ii) Persons	50		
95. Total receipts	205	101. Total payments	205

(10) Appropriation Account

102. Transfer from operating account of surplus	40	107. Payments to depositors actual and imputed	
103. Interest	80	(a) Actual	
104. Dividends	20	(i) Business enterprises	20
105. Insurance claims	5	(ii) Persons	25
		(b) Imputed	
		(i) Business enterprises	5
		(ii) Persons	50
		108. Dividends and withdrawals	25
		109. Direct taxes	10
		110. Transfer to capital and reserve of surplus	10
106. Total receipts	145	111. Total payments	145

(11) CAPITAL AND RESERVE ACCOUNT

112. Transfer from appropriation account of surplus	10	117. Mortgage and similar advances to	
113. Mortgages and similar debts repaid by		(a) Business enterprises	40
(a) Business enterprises	...	(b) Persons	45
(b) Persons	90	118. Net sums deposited with banks and given to banks in return for notes and coin	5
114. Net sums deposited	5		
115. Receipts from redemptions and repayments	5	119. Net purchase of existing securities	15
		120. Subscriptions to new issues	5
116. Total receipts	110	121. Total payments	110

SECTOR III. INSURANCE AND SOCIAL SECURITY AGENCIES

Insurance Companies and Societies

(12) REVENUE ACCOUNTS

(a) Business Enterprises

122. Premiums less commissions to policyholders	115	125. Claims and surrenders	60
123. Imputed charges	5	126. Transfer to reserve account in respect of increase in accruing liability	...
		127. Transfer to operating account of surplus	60
124. Total receipts	120	128. Total payments	120

(b) Persons

129. Premiums less commissions to policyholders	130	133. Claims and surrenders	90
130. Considerations for annuities	45	134. Annuities	30
131. Imputed charges	65	135. Transfer to reserve account in respect of increase in accruing liability	35
		136. Transfer to operating account in respect of surplus	85
132. Total receipts	240	137. Total payments	240

(c) Rest of the World

138. Premiums less commissions to policyholders	10	141. Claims and surrenders	5
139. Imputed charges	...	142. Transfer to reserve account in respect of increase in accruing liability	...
		143. Transfer to operating account of surplus	5
140. Total receipts	10	144. Total payments	10

(13) OPERATING ACCOUNT

145. Transfers from revenue accounts		147. Payments to factors of production	
(a) Business enterprises	60	(a) Wages, salaries, etc.	70
(b) Persons	85	(b) Interest	10
(c) Rest of the world	5	148. Purchases of goods and services	20
		149. Indirect taxes	5
		150. Transfer to appropriation account of surplus	45
146. Total receipts	150	151. Total payments	150

(14) APPROPRIATION ACCOUNT

152. Transfer from operating account of surplus	45	156. Imputed payments to policy-holders	
153. Interest	55	(a) Business enterprises	5
154. Dividends	15	(b) Persons	65
		157. Dividends and withdrawals	20
		158. Direct taxes	15
		159. Transfer to capital and reserve of surplus	10
155. Total receipts	115	160. Total payments	115

(15) CAPITAL AND RESERVE ACCOUNT

161. Transfer from revenue account in respect of excess accruing liability	35	165. Net sums deposited with banks and given to banks in return for notes and coin	5
162. Transfer from appropriation account of surplus	10	166. Net purchase of existing securities	20
163. Receipts from redemptions and repayments	5	167. Subscriptions to new issues	25
164. Total receipts	50	168. Total payments	50

Private Pension Funds

(16) REVENUE ACCOUNT

169. Contributions from employees	20	173. Pension payments	10
170. Interest	5	174. Payments to factors of production	
171. Dividends	...	(a) Wages, salaries, etc.	5
		175. Purchases of goods and services	...
		176. Transfer to reserve account of surplus	10
172. Total receipts	25	177. Total payments	25

(17) RESERVE ACCOUNT

178. Transfer from revenue of surplus	10	180. Net purchase of existing securities	10
179. Total receipts	10	181. Total payments	10

Social Security Funds

(18) REVENUE ACCOUNT

182. Contributions	90	187. Claims and benefits	85
183. Transfer from public collective providers	15	188. Payments to factors of production	
184. Interest	5	(a) Wages, salaries, etc.	10
185. Dividends	...	189. Purchases of goods and services	5
		190. Transfer to reserve account of surplus	10
186. Total receipts	110	191. Total payments	110

(19) RESERVE ACCOUNT

192. Transfer from revenue account of surplus	10	195. Net purchase of existing securities	5
193. Transfer from public collective providers	...	196. Redemption and repayment of obligations	5
194. Total receipts	10	197. Total payments	10

SECTOR IV. FINAL CONSUMERS

Persons

(20) REVENUE ACCOUNT

198. Wages, salaries, etc.	5,460	212. Payments to factors of production	
199. Interest	495	(a) Wages, salaries, etc.	105
200. Receipts, actual and imputed as depositors	255	213. Purchases of goods and services, including bank, etc. charges, actual and imputed, rentals and fees to public collective providers	6,705
201. Imputed receipts as policy-holders	65		
202. Net return from house ownership	165		
203. Dividends and withdrawals	1,505	214. Transfer from operating account of business enterprises in respect of bad debts	−25
204. Transfers from public collective providers	170		
205. Contingency claims	15	215. Insurance premiums	130
206. Insurance claims, surrenders and annuities	120	216. Considerations for annuities	45
207. Pensions from private funds	10	217. Imputed charges to policy-holders	65
208. Social security benefits	85		
209. Gifts from		218. Gifts and fines to	
(a) Persons	70	(a) Persons	70
(b) Rest of the world	45	(b) Public collective providers	5
210. Capital transfers from abroad	15	(c) Rest of the world	20
		219. Direct taxes	745
		220. Contributions to social security funds	45
		221. Contributions to private pension funds	20
		222. Transfers to capital and reserve account of surplus	545
211. Total receipts	8,475	223. Total payments	8,475

(21) CAPITAL AND RESERVE ACCOUNT

224. Transfer from revenue account of surplus	545	229. Payments for factors of production	
225. Bank, mortgage and similar advances	50	(a) Wages, salaries, etc.	50
226. Transfer from house-ownership account in respect of depreciation and obsolescence	50	230. Purchases of goods and services	210
		231. Net purchase of existing assets	...
227. Receipts from redemptions and repayments	5	232. Repayments of advances, mortgages, etc.	90
		233. Net sums deposited with banks and given to banks in return for notes and coin	5
		234. Net sums deposited with other financial intermediaries	5
		235. Net purchase of existing securities	−20
		236. Subscriptions to new issues	310
228. Total receipts	650	237. Total payments	650

Public Collective Providers

(22) REVENUE ACCOUNT

238. Direct taxes	1,080	246. Payments to factors of production	
239. Indirect taxes	405	(a) Wages, salaries, etc.	800
240. Transfer of surplus from appropriation account of publicly controlled enterprises	10	(b) Interest	25
		247. Purchases of goods and services	180
241. Interest	20	248. Contributions to social security funds	15
242. Dividends	...	249. Transfer to social security funds	15
243. Gifts and fines	5	250. Transfers to capital and reserve account in respect of depreciation and obsolescence	45
244. Fees	10	251. Transfer payments (national debt interest)	
		(a) Enterprises	175
		(b) Persons	170
		252. Subsidies	130
		253. Transfer to capital and reserve account of surplus	−25
245. Total receipts	1,530	254. Total payments	1,530

(23) CAPITAL AND RESERVE ACCOUNT

255. Transfer from revenue account of surplus	−25	260. Payments to factors of production	
256. Transfer from revenue of depreciation and obsolescence allowances	45	(a) Wages, salaries, etc.	20
		261. Purchases of goods and services	35
257. Receipts from subscriptions to new securities	10	262. Net purchase of existing assets	−20
		263. Transfer to social security funds	...
258. Receipts from redemptions and repayments	...	264. Net purchase of existing securities	−15
		265. Repayment and redemption of obligations	10
259. Total receipts	30	266. Total payments	30

SECTOR V. REST OF THE WORLD

All Economic Entities

(24) CONSOLIDATED ACCOUNT

267.	Proceeds from sale of factors of production		277.	Payments to factors of production	
	(a) Wages, salaries, etc.	10		(a) Wages, salaries, etc.	15
	(b) Interest	25		(b) Interest	165
268.	Dividends and withdrawals	20	278.	Dividends and withdrawals	60
269.	Proceeds from sale of goods and services including existing equipment, gold, etc.	700	279.	Purchase of goods and services including existing equipment, gold, etc.	505
270.	Insurance premiums	5	280.	Insurance premiums	10
271.	Insurance claims	5	281.	Insurance claims	...
272.	Remittances	20	282.	Remittances	45
273.	Receipts from subscriptions to new issues	25	283.	Capital transfers accompanying persons	15
274.	Other new lending	...	284.	Net sums deposited with banks and given in return for notes and coins	10
275.	Repayments and redemptions	10	285.	Net purchases of existing securities	−25
			286.	Subscriptions to new issues	5
			287.	Repayment and redemption of obligations	15
276.	Total receipts	820	288.	Total payments	820

III

THE ORIGINATING RECONCILIATIONS

SALES PROCEEDS: (1) OPERATING ACCOUNT 1

SECTOR I. Productive enterprises. Business enterprises: (1) Operating account 1. Sales proceeds	...	...	50,000	
SECTOR I. Productive enterprises. Business enterprises: (1) Operating account 6. Purchases of goods and services including bank and similar charges, actual and imputed	...	43,025		
Less SECTOR II. Financial intermediaries. Banking system: (6) Operating account 64. Charges to customers: (a) Actual (i) Business enterprises (b) Imputed (i) Business enterprises	5 25			
Other financial intermediaries: (9) Operating account 94. Charges to customers: (a) Actual (i) Business enterprises (b) Imputed (i) Business enterprises	15 5			
		50	...	42,975
SECTOR I. Productive enterprises. Business enterprises: (3) Capital account 37. Purchases of goods and services	...	...	...	800
Persons (house-ownership): (5) Operating account 58. Purchases of goods and services	...	...	...	45
SECTOR II. Financial intermediaries. Banking system: (6) Operating account 67. Purchases of goods and services	...	...	...	45
Other financial intermediaries: (9) Operating account 97. Purchases of goods and services	...	...	...	30
SECTOR III. Insurance and social security agencies. Insurance companies and societies: (13) Operating account 148. Purchases of goods and services	...	...	...	20
Private pension funds: (16) Revenue account 175. Purchases of goods and services	...	...	...	...
Social security funds: (18) Revenue account 189. Purchases of goods and services	...	...	...	5
SECTOR IV. Final consumers. Persons: (20) Revenue account 213. Purchases of goods and services, including bank, etc. charges, actual and imputed, rentals and fees to public collective providers	...	6,705		
Less SECTOR I. Persons (house-ownership): (5) Operating account 55. Gross rental received or imputed	500			
SECTOR II. Financial intermediaries. Banking system: (6) Operating account 64. Charges to customers: (a) Actual (ii) Persons (b) Imputed (ii) Persons	20 150			
Forward	670	6,705	50,000	43,920

Brought forward	670	6,705	50,000	43,920
Other financial intermediaries:				
(9) Operating account 94. Charges to customers:				
(a) Actual (ii) Persons	135			
(b) Imputed (ii) Persons	50			
SECTOR IV. Final consumers: public collective providers:				
(22) Revenue account 244. Fees	10			
		865	...	5,840
Final consumers. Persons:				
(21) Capital and reserve account 230. Purchases of goods and services	...	...	...	210
Public collective providers:				
(22) Revenue account 247. Purchases of goods and services	...	...	...	180
(23) Capital and reserve account 261. Purchases of goods and services	...	...	...	35
SECTOR V. Rest of the world. All economic entities:				
(24) Consolidated account 279. Purchases of goods and services	...	...	...	500[1]
				50,685
Deduct SECTOR V. Rest of the world. All economic entities:				
(24) Consolidated account 269. Sales of goods and services	...	...	...	685[2]
Total			50,000	50,000

[1] Included in the payment of 505 attributed to purchases of goods and services including existing equipment, gold, etc.

[2] Included in the receipt of 700 attributed to proceeds from sale of goods and services including existing equipment, gold, etc.

SUBSIDIES: (1) OPERATING ACCOUNT 2

SECTOR I. Productive enterprises. Business enterprises:		
(1) Operating account 2. Subsidies	130	
SECTOR IV. Final consumers. Public collective providers:		
(22) Revenue account 252. Subsidies	...	130
	130	130

UNSOLD GOODS, WORK IN PROGRESS AND UNUSED MATERIALS: (1) OPERATING ACCOUNT 3

SECTOR I. Productive enterprises. Business enterprises:		
(1) Operating account 3. Transfer from capital account in respect of unsold goods, work in progress and unused materials	70	
SECTOR I. (3) Capital account 39. Transfer to operating account in respect of unsold goods, work in progress and unused materials	...	70
	70	70

PAYMENTS TO FACTORS OF PRODUCTION, WAGES, SALARIES, ETC.:
(1) OPERATING ACCOUNT 5 (*a*)

SECTOR I. Productive enterprises. Business enterprises:		
(1) Operating account 5. Payments to factors of production:		
(*a*) Wages, salaries, etc.	...	3,975
SECTOR IV. Final consumers. Persons:		
(20) Revenue account 198. Wages, salaries, etc.	3,975[1]	
	3,975	3,975

[1] Included in the receipt of 5,460 attributed to wages, salaries, etc.

INTEREST

SECTOR I. Productive enterprises. Business enterprises:		
(1) Operating account 5. Payments to factors of production:		
(*b*) Interest	...	500
Persons (house-ownership):		
(5) Operating account 57:		
(*b*) Interest	...	20
SECTOR III. Insurance and social security agencies. Insurance companies and societies:		
(13) Operating account 147. Payments to factors of production:		
(*b*) Interest	...	10
SECTOR IV. Final consumers. Public collective providers:		
(22) Revenue account 246. Payments to factors of production:		
(*b*) Interest	...	25
(22) Revenue account 251. Transfer payments (national debt interest):		
(*a*) Enterprises	...	175
(*b*) Persons	...	170
SECTOR V. Rest of the world. All economic entities:		
(24) Consolidated account 277. Payments to factors of production:		
(*b*) Interest	...	165
SECTOR I. Productive enterprises. Business enterprises:		
(2) Appropriation account 16. Interest	10	
SECTOR II. Financial intermediaries. Banking system:		
(7) Appropriation account 73. Interest	200	
Other financial intermediaries:		
(10) Appropriation account 103. Interest	80	
SECTOR III. Insurance and social security agencies. Insurance companies and societies:		
(14) Appropriation account 153. Interest	55	
Private pensions funds:		
(16) Revenue account 170. Interest	5	
Social security funds:		
(18) Revenue account 184. Interest	5	
SECTOR IV. Final consumers. Persons:		
(20) Revenue account 199. Interest	495	
(20) Revenue account 204. Transfers from public collective providers	170	
Public collective providers:		
(22) Revenue account 241. Interest	20	
SECTOR V. Rest of the world. All economic entities:		
(24) Consolidated account 267. Proceeds from sale of factors of production:		
(*b*) Interest	25	
	1,065	1,065

PURCHASES OF GOODS AND SERVICES: (1) OPERATING ACCOUNT 6

SECTOR I. Productive enterprises. Business enterprises:			
(1) Operating account 6. Purchases of goods and services including bank and similar charges, actual and imputed	...	...	43,025
SECTOR I. Productive enterprises. Business enterprises:			
(1) Operating account 1. Sales proceeds	...	42,975[1]	
SECTOR II. Financial intermediaries. Banking system:			
(6) Operating account 64. Charges to customers:			
(a) Actual (i) Business enterprises	5		
Other financial intermediaries:			
(9) Operating account 94. Charges to customers:			
(a) Actual (i) Business enterprises.	15		
Financial intermediaries. Banking system:		20	
(6) Operating account 64. Charges to customers:			
(b) Imputed (i) Business enterprises	25		
Other financial intermediaries:			
(9) Operating account 94. Charges to customers:			
(b) Imputed (i) Business enterprises	5		
		30	
		43,025	43,025

[1] Included in the receipt of 50,000 attributed to sales proceeds. See the originating reconciliation for this item.

INSURANCE PREMIUMS AND IMPUTED CHARGES TO POLICYHOLDERS: (1) OPERATING ACCOUNT 7

SECTOR I. Productive enterprises. Business enterprises:		
(1) Operating account 7:		
Insurance premiums	...	75
Imputed charges to policyholders	...	5
SECTOR III. Insurance and social security agencies. Insurance companies and societies:		
(12) Revenue accounts:		
(a) Business enterprises:		
122. Premiums less commissions to policyholders	75[1]	
123. Imputed charges	5	
	80	80

[1] Included in the receipt of 115 attributed to premiums less commissions to policyholders.

INSURANCE PREMIUMS AND IMPUTED CHARGES TO POLICYHOLDERS
(ENTERPRISES)

	Imputed		Actual	
SECTOR I. Productive enterprises. Business enterprises:				
(1) Operating account 7:				
Insurance premiums	...	...	...	75
Imputed charges to policyholders	...	5		
Persons (house-ownership):				
(5) Operating account 59. Insurance premiums	...	...	...	30
SECTOR II. Financial intermediaries. Banking system:				
(6) Operating account 68. Insurance premiums	...	...	...	5
Other financial intermediaries:				
(9) Operating account 98. Insurance premiums	...	...	...	10
SECTOR III. Insurance and social security agencies. Insurance companies and societies:				
(12) Revenue accounts:				
(a) Business enterprises:				
122. Premiums less commissions to policyholders	...	...	115	
123. Imputed charges	5			
	5	5	115	120
Deduct SECTOR V. Rest of the world. All economic entities:				
(24) Consolidated account 270. Insurance premiums	...	...	...	5
	5	5	115	115

INDIRECT TAXES: (1) OPERATING ACCOUNT 8

SECTOR I. Productive enterprises. Business enterprises:		
(1) Operating account 8. Indirect taxes	...	270
SECTOR IV. Final consumers. Public collective providers:		
(22) Revenue account 239. Indirect taxes	270[1]	
	270	270

[1] Included in the receipt of 405 attributed to indirect taxes.

CONTRIBUTIONS TO SOCIAL SECURITY FUNDS: (1) OPERATING ACCOUNT 9

SECTOR I. Productive enterprises. Business enterprises:		
(1) Operating account 9. Contributions to social security funds	...	30
SECTOR III. Insurance and social security agencies. Social security funds:		
(18) Revenue account 182. Contributions	30[1]	
	30	30

[1] Included in the receipt of 90 attributed to contributions.

INVENTORIES TAKEN OVER: (1) OPERATING ACCOUNT 10

SECTOR I. Productive enterprises. Business enterprises:		
(1) Operating account 10. Transfer to capital account in respect of inventories taken over	...	55
SECTOR I. Productive enterprises. Business enterprises:		
(3) Capital account 31. Transfer from operating account in resepect of inventories taken over	55	
	55	55

Transfer to Capital Account in Respect of Depreciation and Obsolescence: (1) Operating Account 11

Sector I. Productive enterprises. Business enterprises:		
(1) Operating account 11. Transfer to capital account in respect of depreciation and obsolescence	...	440
Sector I. Productive enterprises. Business enterprises:		
(3) Capital account 32. Transfer from operating account in respect of depreciation and obsolescence	440	
	440	440

Transfer to Revenue Account of Persons in Respect of Bad Debts: (1) Operating Account 12

Sector I. Productive enterprises. Business enterprises:		
(1) Operating account 12. Transfer to revenue account of persons in respect of bad debts	...	25
Sector IV. Final consumers. Persons:		
(20) Revenue account 214. Transfer from operating account of business enterprises in respect of bad debts	...	−25
	...	0

Transfer to Appropriation Account of Surplus: (1) Operating Account 13

Sector I. Productive enterprises. Business enterprises:		
(1) Operating account 13. Transfer to appropriation account of surplus	...	1,800
Sector I. Business enterprises:		
(2) Appropriation account 15. Transfer from operating account of surplus	1,800	
	1,800	1,800

Receipts in Respect of Deposits Actual and Imputed: (2) Appropriation Account 17

Sector I. Productive enterprises. Business enterprises:		
(2) Appropriation account 17. Receipts in respect of deposits actual (65) and imputed (30)	95	
Sector II. Financial intermediaries. Banking system:		
(7) Appropriation account 77. Payments to depositors actual and imputed:		
(a) Actual (i) Business enterprises	...	45
(b) Imputed (i) Business enterprises	...	25
Other financial intermediaries:		
(10) Appropriation account 107. Payments to depositors actual and imputed:		
(a) Actual (i) Business enterprises	...	20
(b) Imputed (i) Business enterprises	...	5
	95	95

IMPUTED RECEIPTS AS POLICYHOLDERS: (2) APPROPRIATION ACCOUNT 18

SECTOR I. Productive enterprises. Business enterprises:		
(2) Appropriation account 18. Imputed receipts as policyholders	5	
SECTOR III. Insurance and social security agencies. Insurance companies and societies:		
(14) Appropriation account 156. Imputed payments to policyholders:		
(a) Business enterprises	...	5
	5	5

DIVIDENDS AND WITHDRAWALS

SECTOR I. Productive enterprises. Business enterprises:		
(2) Appropriation account 19	120	
SECTOR II. Financial intermediaries. Banking system		
(7) Appropriation account 74	50	
Other financial intermediaries:		
(10) Appropriation account 104	20	
SECTOR III. Insurance and social security agencies. Insurance companies and societies:		
(14) Appropriation account 154	15	
SECTOR IV. Final consumers. Persons:		
(20) Revenue account 203	1,505	
Public collective providers:		
(22) Revenue account 240	10	
SECTOR V. Rest of the world. All economic entities:		
(24) Consolidated account 268	20	
SECTOR I. Productive enterprises. Business enterprises:		
(2) Appropriation account 24	...	1,600
SECTOR II. Financial intermediaries. Banking system:		
(7) Appropriation account 78	...	35
Other financial intermediaries:		
(10) Appropriation account 108	...	25
SECTOR III. Insurance and social security agencies. Insurance companies and societies:		
(14) Appropriation account 157	...	20
SECTOR V. Rest of the world. All economic entities:		
(24) Consolidated account 278	...	60
	1,740	1,740

INSURANCE CLAIMS: (2) APPROPRIATION ACCOUNT 20

SECTOR I. Productive enterprises. Business enterprises:		
(2) Appropriation account 20. Insurance claims	55	
SECTOR II. Financial intermediaries. Other financial intermediaries:		
(10) Appropriation account 105. Insurance claims	5	
SECTOR III. Insurance and social security agencies. Insurance companies and societies:		
(12) Revenue accounts:		
(a) Business enterprises. 125 Claims and surrenders	...	60
	60	60

Transfer from Reserve in Respect of Excess Provision for Taxation: (2) Appropriation Account 21

Sector I. Productive enterprises. Business enterprises:		
(2) Appropriation account 21. Transfer from reserve in respect of excess provision for taxation	5	
Sector I. Productive enterprises. Business enterprises:		
(4) Reserve account 47. Transfer to appropriation account in respect of excess provision for taxation	...	5
	5	5

Transfer from Reserve in Respect of Realised Capital Gains: (2) Appropriation Account 22

Sector I. Productive enterprises. Business enterprises:		
(2) Appropriation account 22. Transfer from reserve in respect of realised capital gains	15	
Sector I. Productive enterprises. Business enterprises:		
(4) Reserve account 48. Transfer to appropriation account in respect of realised capital gains	...	15
	15	15

Direct Taxes: (2) Appropriation Account 25

Sector I. Productive enterprises. Business enterprises:		
(2) Appropriation account 25. Direct taxes	...	300
Sector IV. Public collective providers:		
(22) Revenue account 238. Direct taxes	300[1]	
	300	300

[1] Included in the receipt of 1,080 attributed to direct taxes.

Payments of Contingency Claims to Employees and Third Parties: (2) Appropriation Account 26

Sector I. Productive enterprises. Business enterprises:		
(2) Appropriation account 26. Payments of contingency claims to employees and third parties	...	15
Sector IV. Final consumers. Persons		
(20) Revenue account 205. Contingency claims	15	
	15	15

Transfer to Reserve in Respect of Unpaid Accruing Tax Liability: (2) Appropriation Account 28

Sector I. Productive enterprises. Business enterprises:		
(2) Appropriation account 28. Transfer to reserve in respect of unpaid accruing tax liability	...	45
Sector I. Productive enterprises. Business enterprises:		
(4) Reserve account 41. Transfer from appropriation account in respect of unpaid accruing tax liability	45	
	45	45

PAYMENTS TO FACTORS OF PRODUCTION, WAGES, SALARIES, ETC.:
(3) CAPITAL ACCOUNT 36 (a)

SECTOR I. Productive enterprises. Business enterprises:		
(3) Capital account 36. Payments to factors of production:		
(a) Wages, salaries, etc.	...	135
SECTOR IV. Final consumers. Persons:		
(20) Revenue account 198	135[1]	
	135	135

[1] Included in the receipt of 5,460 attributed to wages, salaries, etc.

PURCHASES OF GOODS AND SERVICES: (3) CAPITAL ACCOUNT 37

SECTOR I. Productive enterprises. Business enterprises:		
(3) Capital account 37. Purchases of goods and services	...	800
SECTOR I. Productive enterprises. Business enterprises:		
(1) Operating account 1. Sales proceeds	800[1]	
	800	800

[1] Mainly included in the receipt of 50,000 attributed to sales proceeds. See the originating reconciliation for this item.

NET PURCHASES OF EXISTING EQUIPMENT AND OTHER ASSETS:
(3) CAPITAL ACCOUNT 38

SECTOR I. Productive enterprises. Business enterprises:		
(3) Capital account 38. Net purchases of existing equipment and other assets	...	15
SECTOR V. Rest of the world. All economic entities:		
(24) Consolidated account 269. Proceeds from sale of existing equipment	15[1]	
	15	15

[1] Included in the receipt of 700 attributed to proceeds from sale of goods and services including existing equipment, gold, etc.

RECEIPTS FROM SUBSCRIPTIONS TO NEW ISSUES, ETC.:
(4) RESERVE ACCOUNT 43

SECTOR I. Productive enterprises. Business enterprises:		
(4) Reserve account 43. Receipts from subscriptions to new issues, etc.	345	
(4) Reserve account 51. Subscriptions to new issues, etc.	...	5
SECTOR II. Financial intermediaries. Banking system:		
(8) Capital and reserve account 84	5	
(8) Capital and reserve account 90	...	35
Other financial intermediaries:		
(11) Capital and reserve account 120	...	5
SECTOR III. Insurance and social security agencies. Insurance companies and societies:		
(15) Capital and reserve account 167	...	25
SECTOR IV. Final consumers. Persons:		
(21) Capital and reserve account 236	...	310
Public collective providers:		
(23) Capital and reserve account 257	10	
SECTOR V. Rest of the world. All economic entities:		
(24) Consolidated account 273	25	
(24) Consolidated account 286	...	5
	385	385

OTHER NEW BORROWING: (4) RESERVE ACCOUNT 44

SECTOR I. Productive enterprises. Business enterprises:		
(4) Reserve account 44. Other new borrowing from:		
(a) Banks	25	
(b) Other financial intermediaries	40	
SECTOR II. Financial intermediaries. Banking system:		
(8) Capital and reserve account 89. Discounts and advances to		
(a) Business enterprises	...	25
Other financial intermediaries:		
(11) Capital and reserve account 117. Mortgage and similar advances to		
(a) Business enterprises	...	40
	65	65

REDEMPTIONS AND REPAYMENTS

SECTOR I. Productive enterprises. Business enterprises:		
(4) Reserve account 45. Receipts from redemptions and repayments	15	
(4) Reserve account 53. Redemption and repayment of obligations	...	20
SECTOR II. Financial intermediaries. Banking system:		
(8) Capital and reserve account 85	10	
Other financial intermediaries:		
(11) Capital and reserve account 115	5	
SECTOR III. Insurance companies and societies:		
(15) Capital and reserve account 163	5	
Social security funds:		
(19) Reserve account 196	...	5
SECTOR IV. Final consumers. Persons:		
(21) Capital and reserve account 227	5	
Public collective providers:		
(23) Capital and reserve account 265	...	10
SECTOR V. Rest of the world. All economic entities:		
(24) Consolidated account 275	10	
(24) Consolidated account 287	...	15
	50	50

NET SUMS DEPOSITED WITH BANKS AND GIVEN IN RETURN
FOR NOTES AND COIN

SECTOR I. Productive enterprises. Business enterprises:		
(4) Reserve account 50. Net sums deposited with banks and given in return for notes and coin	...	40
SECTOR II. Financial intermediaries. Banking system:		
(8) Capital and reserve account 83. Net sums deposited and received in return for notes and coin	65	
Other financial intermediaries:		
(11) Capital and reserve account 118	...	5
SECTOR III. Insurance companies and societies:		
(15) Capital and reserve account 165	...	5
SECTOR IV. Final consumers. Persons:		
(21) Capital and reserve account 233	...	5
SECTOR V. Rest of the world. All economic entities:		
(24) Consolidated account 284	...	10
	65	65

NET PURCHASES OF EXISTING SECURITIES

	(+)	(−)
SECTOR I. Productive enterprises. Business enterprises:		
(4) Reserve account 52	5	
SECTOR II. Financial intermediaries. Banking system:		
(8) Capital and reserve account 91	5	
Other financial intermediaries:		
(11) Capital and reserve account 119	15	
SECTOR III. Insurance companies and societies:		
(15) Capital and reserve account 166	20	
Private pensions funds:		
(17) Reserve account 180	10	
Social security funds:		
(19) Reserve account 195	5	
SECTOR IV. Final consumers. Persons:		
(21) Capital and reserve account 235	...	20
Public collective providers:		
(23) Capital and reserve account 264	...	15
SECTOR V. Rest of the world. All economic entities:		
(24) Consolidated account 285	...	25
	60	60

IV

THE PRIMARY RECONCILIATIONS

SALES (1) 1

Reference to source of sale				Receivables
SECTOR I. Other business enterprises:				
(1) Operating account 6. Sales proceeds	47,365			
Less Opening debtors and accrued revenues[1]	8,860			
		38,505		
Add Closing debtors and accrued revenues[1]		4,470		
			42,975	
(3) Capital account 37. Sales proceeds	854			
Less Opening debtors	100			
		754		
Add Closing debtors		46		
			800	
(5) Operating account 58. Sales proceeds	45			
Less Opening debtors	...			
		45		
Add Closing debtors		...		
			45	
SECTOR II. Financial intermediaries. Banking system:				
(6) Operating account 67. Sales proceeds	45			
Less Opening debtors	...			
		45		
Add Closing debtors		...		
			45	
Other financial intermediaries:				
(9) Operating account 97. Sales proceeds	30			
Less Opening debtors	...			
		30		
Add Closing debtors		...		
			30	
SECTOR III. Insurance and social security agencies. Insurance companies and societies:				
(13) Operating account 148. Sales proceeds	20			
Less Opening debtors	...			
		20		
Add Closing debtors		...		
			20	
Private pension funds:				
(16) Revenue account 175. Sales proceeds	...			
Less Opening debtors	...			
		...		
Add Closing debtors		...		
			...	
Social security funds:				
(18) Revenue account 189. Sales proceeds	5			
Less Opening debtors	...			
		5		
Add Closing debtors		...		
			5	
Forward			43,920	

[1] Accrued revenues (calculated on a time basis) will also apply to other items which include services rendered and paid for on a time basis.

Reference to source of sale		Receivables
Brought forward		43,920
SECTOR IV. Final consumers. Persons:		
(20) Revenue account 213. Sales proceeds	6,070	
Less Opening debtors	500	
	5,570	
Add Closing debtors	270	
		5,840
(21) Capital and reserve account 230. Sales proceeds	220	
Less Opening debtors	20	
	200	
Add Closing debtors	10	
		210
Public collective providers:		
(22) Revenue account 247. Sales proceeds	188	
Less Opening debtors	15	
	173	
Add Closing debtors	7	
		180
(23) Capital and reserve account 261. Sales proceeds	36	
Less Opening debtors	5	
	31	
Add Closing debtors	4	
		35
SECTOR V. Rest of the world. All economic entities:		
(24) Consolidated account 279. Sales proceeds	807	
Less Opening debtors	500	
	307	
Add Closing debtors	193	
		500
		50,685
Deduct SECTOR V. Rest of the world. All economic entities:		
(24) Consolidated account 269	...	...	685
		50,000

PURCHASES OF GOODS AND SERVICES: (1) OPERATING ACCOUNT 6

Reference to source of purchase		Payables
SECTOR I. Other business enterprises:		
(1) Operating account 1. Payments for purchases of goods and services	47,365	
Less Opening creditors and accrued expenses (calculated on a time basis)	8,860	
Payments for current purchases of goods and services	...	38,505
Add Closing creditors and accrued expenses (calculated on a time basis)	4,470	
Say Creditors	4,000	
Accrued expenses	470	
	4,470	
		42,975

INDIRECT TAXES: (1) OPERATING ACCOUNT 8 (ORIGINATING STRUCTURE);
7 (REVISED STRUCTURE)

Reference to destination of tax	Payables	
SECTOR IV. Final consumers. Public collective providers:		
(22) Revenue account 239. Opening provision for unexpired payments in respect of such items as registration licences, local rates, etc. (calculated on a time basis)	37	
Payments for indirect taxes	273	
	310	
Deduct Closing provision for unexpired payments (calculated on a time basis)	40	270

PAYABLES TO FACTORS OF PRODUCTION: (1) OPERATING ACCOUNT 5
(ORIGINATING STRUCTURE); 8 (REVISED STRUCTURE)

(a) Wages, salaries, etc.

Reference to destination	Payables	
SECTOR IV. Final consumers. Persons:		
(20) Revenue account 198. Payments for wages, salaries, etc.	3,965	
Deduct Opening provision for accrued wages and salaries (calculated on a time basis)	65	
	3,900	
Add Closing provision for accrued wages and salaries (calculated on a time basis)	75	3,975

PAYABLES TO FACTORS OF PRODUCTION: (1) OPERATING ACCOUNT 5
(ORIGINATING STRUCTURE); 8 (REVISED STRUCTURE)

(b) Interest

Reference to destination	Payables	
SECTOR I. Productive enterprises. Other business enterprises:		
(2) Appropriation account 16		
SECTOR II. Financial intermediaries. Banking system:		
(7) Appropriation account 73. Other financial intermediaries		
(10) Appropriation account 103		
SECTOR III. Insurance and social security agencies. Insurance companies and societies:		
(14) Appropriation account 13		
SECTOR IV. Final consumers. Persons:		
(20) Revenue account 199		
SECTOR V. Rest of the world. All economic entities:		
(24) Consolidated account 267		
Payments for interest on borrowed money	510	
Deduct Opening provision for accrued interest (calculated on a time basis)	30	
	480	
Add Closing provision for accrued interest (calculated on a time basis)	20	500

INTEREST

	Payments	−Opening provision for accrued interest (creditor) (calculated on a time basis)		+Closing provision for accrued interest (creditor) (calculated on a time basis)	Payables
SECTOR I. Productive enterprises. Business enterprises:					
(1) Operating account 8(b) Persons (house-ownership):	510	30	480	20	500
(5) Operating account 57:	19	2	17	3	20
SECTOR III. Insurance and social security agencies. Insurance companies and societies:					
(13) Operating account 147:	11	2	9	1	10
SECTOR IV. Final consumers. Public collective providers:					
(22) Revenue account 246:	24	3	21	4	25
251. Transfer payments (national debt interest):					
(a) Enterprises	175	...	175	...	175 Transfer payments
(b) Persons	170	...	170	...	170 Transfer payments
SECTOR V. Rest of the world. All economic entities:					
(24) Consolidated account 277:	168	15	153	12	165
	1,077	52	1,025	40	1,065

INTEREST

	Receipts	− Opening provision for accrued interest (debtor) (calculated on a time basis)		+ Closing provision for accrued interest (debtor) (calculated on a time basis)	Receivables
SECTOR I. Productive enterprises. Business enterprises:					
(2) Appropriation account 16	11	3	8	2	10
SECTOR II. Financial intermediaries. Banking system:					
(7) Appropriation account 73	213	19	194	6	200
Other financial intermediaries:					
(10) Appropriation account 103	81	5	76	4	80
SECTOR III. Insurance and social security agencies. Insurance companies and societies:					
(14) Appropriation account 153	57	4	53	2	55
Private pensions funds:					
(16) Revenue account 170	5	…	5	…	5
Social security funds:					
(18) Revenue account 184	5	…	5	…	5
SECTOR IV. Final consumers. Persons:					
(20) Revenue account 199	490	17	473	22	495
204. Transfers from public collective providers (national debt interest)	170	…	170	…	170 (Transfer receipts)
Public collective providers:					
(22) Revenue account 241	19	1	18	2	20
SECTOR V. Rest of the world. All economic entities:					
(24) Consolidated account 267 (b)	26	3	23	2	25
	1,077	52	1,025	40	1,065

PROVISION FOR DEPRECIATION AND OBSOLESCENCE

SECTOR I. Productive enterprises. Business enterprises:
(1) 11. (Originating structure)
     10. (Revised structure)
Depreciation and obsolescence. Aggregated profit-and-loss account. Operating
    section. Payables. The accounting convention. Arithmetical allocation
    based on original cost   300
Assumed adjustment in a period of rising prices
Management replacement adjustment. Aggregated profit-and-loss account.
    Operating section. Payables (retained in this account to preserve the
    economic conception of operating surplus)   +140

                                                                                    440

INSURANCE PREMIUMS: (1) OPERATING ACCOUNT 7 (ORIGINATING
STRUCTURE); 11 (REVISED STRUCTURE)

Reference to destination		Payables
SECTOR III. Insurance and social security agencies. Insurance companies and societies:		
(12) Revenue Accounts:		
(a) Business enterprises 122		
Opening provision for unexpired premium payments (calculated on a time basis)	5	
Insurance premium payments	76	
	81	
Deduct Closing provision for unexpired premium payments (calculated on a time basis)	6	
		75

INSURANCE PREMIUMS

	Opening provisions for unexpired premium payments (debtor) (calculated on a time basis)	+ Premium payments made during the accounting period		− Closing provisions for unexpired premium payments (debtor) (calculated on a time basis)	Payables
SECTOR I. Productive enterprises. Business enterprises:					
(1) Operating account 11	5	76	81	6	75
Persons (house-ownership):					
(5) Operating account 59	3	31	34	4	30
SECTOR II. Financial intermediaries. Banking system:					
(6) Operating account 68	2	4	6	1	5
Other financial intermediaries:					
(9) Operating account 98	3	9	12	2	10
	13	120	133	13	120
Deduct SECTOR V. Rest of the world. All economic entities:					
(24) Consolidated account 270	...	5	5	...	5
	13	115	128	13	115

	Opening provisions for unexpired premiums (creditor) (calculated on a time basis)	+ Premium receipts during the accounting period	− Closing provisions for unexpired premiums (creditor) (calculated on a time basis)	Receivables
SECTOR III. Insurance and social security agencies. Insurance companies and societies:				
(12) Revenue accounts:				
(a) Business enterprises 122	13	128	13	115

INTEREST: (2) AGGREGATED PROFIT-AND-LOSS ACCOUNT.
NON-OPERATING SECTION 16

	Receipts during the accounting period	−Opening provision for accrued interest (debtor) (calculated on a time basis)	+Closing provision for accrued interest (debtor) (calculated on a time basis)	Receivables
SECTOR I. Business enterprises:				
(2) Non-operating account:				
16 (a) Interest	6	3	3	2	5
16 (b) Transfers from public collective providers— national debt interest	5	...	5	...	5
	11	3	8	2	10

CONSEQUENTIAL LOSS INSURANCE CLAIMS: (2) AGGREGATED
PROFIT-AND-LOSS ACCOUNT. NON-OPERATING SECTION 22

	Payables	Receivables
SECTOR I. Business enterprises:		
(2) Non-operating account 22. Consequential loss insurance claims	...	20
SECTOR I. Business enterprises:		
(3) Capital account 33	...	35
SECTOR II. Financial intermediaries. Other financial intermediaries:		
(10) Appropriation account 105	...	5
SECTOR III. Insurance and social security agencies. Insurance companies and societies:		
(12) Revenue accounts:		
(a) Business enterprises 125	60	...
	60	60

PUBLIC COLLECTIVE PROVIDERS: (2) AGGREGATED PROFIT-AND-LOSS
ACCOUNT. NON-OPERATING SECTION 26

	Payables	Receivables
SECTOR I. Business enterprises:		
(2) Non-operating account 26. Public collective providers. Transfer of operating surplus applicable to publicly controlled enterprises	10	
SECTOR IV. Public collective providers:		
(22) Revenue account 240. Transfer of surplus from publicly controlled enterprises	...	10
	10	10

PURCHASES OF GOODS AND SERVICES ON CAPITAL ACCOUNT

Reference to source of purchase		Payables
SECTOR I. Business enterprises:		
(1) Operating account 1. Payments for purchases of goods and services on capital account	854	
Deduct Creditors at beginning of accounting period	100	
	754	
Add Creditors at close of accounting period	46	
		800

DIVIDENDS (BEFORE DEDUCTION OF INCOME TAX) AND WITHDRAWALS:
(3) APPROPRIATION ACCOUNT 31 (REVISED STRUCTURE)

Reference to destination		Payables
SECTOR I. Productive enterprises. Business enterprises:		
(2) Non-operating account 17 (Revised structure)		
SECTOR II. Financial intermediaries. Banking system:		
(7) Appropriation account 74		
Other financial intermediaries:		
(10) Appropriation account 104		
SECTOR III. Insurance and social security agencies. Insurance companies and societies:		
(14) Appropriation account 154		
SECTOR IV. Final consumers. Persons:		
(20) Revenue account 203		
SECTOR V. Rest of the world. All economic entities:		
(24) Consolidated account 268		
Dividend payments (before deduction of income tax) and withdrawals	1,580	
Deduct Proposed dividends (before deduction of income tax) at the beginning of the accounting period	20	
	1,560	
Add Proposed dividends (before deduction of income tax) at the close of the accounting period	30	
		1,590

V

THE OPENING AND CLOSING CIRCULATING CAPITAL FUNDS

CIRCULATING CAPITAL FUND AT BEGINNING OF ACCOUNTING PERIOD

	Dr.	Cr.
(1) 1. SALES. Debtors at beginning of accounting period for goods delivered or services rendered and invoiced or charged but not paid for during the immediately preceding accounting period, and accrued revenues calculated on a time basis		
SECTOR I. Other business enterprises:		
(1) Operating account 6	8,860	
(3) Capital account 37	100	
Persons (house-ownership):		
(5) Operating account 58	...	
		8,960
SECTOR II. Financial intermediaries. Banking system:		
(6) Operating account 67	...	
Other financial intermediaries:		
(9) Operating account 97	...	
		—
SECTOR III. Insurance and social security agencies. Insurance companies and societies:		
(13) Operating account 148	...	
Private pension funds:		
(16) Revenue account 175	...	
Social security funds:		
(18) Revenue account 189	...	
		—
SECTOR IV. Final consumers. Persons:		
(20) Revenue account 213	500	
(21) Capital and reserve account 230	20	
Public collective providers:		
(22) Revenue account 247	15	
(23) Capital and reserve account 261	5	
		540
SECTOR V. Rest of the world. All economic entities:		
(24) Consolidated account 279		500
		10,000
(1) 10. (Originating structure)		
5. (Revised structure)		
INVENTORIES at beginning of accounting period in respect of unused materials, work in progress or process, and unsold goods		
Set at the conventional accounting valuation adopted at the close of the immediately preceding accounting period		55
(1) 6. PURCHASES. Creditors at beginning of accounting period for goods delivered or services rendered and invoiced or charged but not paid for during the immediately preceding accounting period, and accrued expenses calculated on a time basis	8,860	
Forward	8,860	10,055

	Dr.	Cr.
Brought forward	8,860	10,055
(1) 8. (Originating structure) 7. (Revised structure) INDIRECT TAXES. Provision at beginning of accounting period for unexpired payments in respect of such items as registration licences, local rates, etc. (calculated on a time basis)		37
(1) 5. (Originating structure) 8. (Revised structure) PAYABLES TO FACTORS OF PRODUCTION: (a) Wages, salaries, etc. Provision at beginning of accounting period for accrued wages and salaries (calculated on a time basis)	65	
(b) Interest. Provision at beginning of accounting period for accrued interest on borrowed money (calculated on a time basis)	30	
(1) 7. (Originating structure) 11. (Revised structure) INSURANCE PREMIUMS. Provision at beginning of accounting period for unexpired premium payments (calculated on a time basis)		5
(2) 16. INTEREST (receivable). Provision at beginning of accounting period for accrued interest (calculated on a time basis)		3
(2) 21. (Originating structure) 24. (Revised structure) TAXATION. Over provision treated as a current liability at beginning of accounting period	5	
(2) 24. (Originating structure) (3) 31. (Revised structure) DIVIDENDS (before deduction of income tax). Proposed dividends at beginning of the accounting period	20	
(3) 37. (Originating structure) PURCHASES OF GOODS AND SERVICES on capital account. Creditors at beginning of accounting period for goods delivered or services rendered and invoiced or charged but not paid for during the immediately preceding accounting period	100	
Circulating capital fund at beginning of accounting period per balance statement and resting account	1,020	
	10,100	10,100

Analysis of Fund

	Dr.	Cr.
1. Opening inventories	...	55
Debtors and unexpired payments	10,045	
Creditors and accruals	9,080	
2. Net debtors	...	965
3. Money resources	...	Nil
		1,020

CIRCULATING CAPITAL FUND AT CLOSE OF ACCOUNTING PERIOD

	Dr.	Cr.
1. (1) SALES. Debtors at close of accounting period for goods delivered or services rendered and invoiced or charged but not paid for during this period, and accrued revenues (calculated on a time basis)		
SECTOR I. Other business enterprises:		
(1) Operating account 6	4,470	
(3) Capital account 37	46	
Persons (house-ownership):		
(5) Operating account 58	...	
		4,516
SECTOR II. Financial intermediaries. Banking system:		
(6) Operating account 67	...	
Other financial intermediaries:		
(9) Operating account 97	...	
		...
SECTOR III. Insurance and social security agencies. Insurance companies and societies:		
(13) Operating account 148	...	
Private pension funds:		
(16) Revenue account 175	...	
Social security funds:		
(18) Revenue account 189	...	...
SECTOR IV. Final consumers. Persons:		
(20) Revenue account 213	270	
(21) Capital and reserve account 230	10	
Public collective providers:		
(22) Revenue account 247	7	
(23) Capital and reserve account 261	4	
		291
SECTOR V. Rest of the world. All economic entities:		
(24) Consolidated account 279	193	
3. (1) INVENTORIES at close of accounting period in respect of unused materials, work in progress or process, and unsold goods. Calculated by reference to opening inventory prices	65	
Adjustment to accord with conventional accounting valuation	5	
		70
6. (1) PURCHASES. Creditors at close of accounting period for goods delivered or services rendered and invoiced or charged but not paid for during the immediately preceding accounting period, and accrued expenses calculated on a time basis £4,470		
Say		
Creditors		4,000
Accrued expenses		470
7. (1) INDIRECT TAXES. Unexpired payments at close of accounting period in respect of such items as registration licences, local rates, etc. (calculated on a time basis)	40	
8. (1) PAYABLES TO FACTORS OF PRODUCTION:		
(a) Wages, salaries, etc.		
Provision at close of accounting period for accrued wages and salaries (calculated on a time basis)		75
(b) Interest on borrowed money		
Provision at close of accounting period for accrued interest on borrowed money (calculated on a time basis)		20
Forward	5,110	4,565

	Dr.	Cr.
Brought forward	5,110	4,565
11. (1) INSURANCE PREMIUMS. Unexpired premium payments at close of accounting period (calculated on a time basis)	6	
16(a). (2) INTEREST RECEIVABLE. Provision at close of accounting period for accrued interest (debtor) (calculated on a time basis)	2	
31. (3) DIVIDENDS (before deduction of income tax). Proposed dividends at close of accounting period (creditor)		30
(3) 37. (Originating structure.) PURCHASES OF GOODS AND SERVICES on capital account Creditors at close of accounting period for goods delivered or services rendered and invoiced or charged but not paid for during the immediately preceding accounting period		46
	5,118	4,641
Increase in money resources per accompanying receipts and payments account	618	
Circulating capital fund at close of accounting period per resting account		1,095
	5,736	5,736

Analysis of Fund

	Dr.	Cr.
1. Closing inventories:		
At opening inventory prices	65	
Adjustment to accord with conventional accounting valuation	5	
		70
Debtors and unexpired payments	5,048	
Creditors and accruals	4,641	
2. Net debtors		407
3. Money resources		618
		1,095

MOVEMENTS IN MONETARY RESOURCES

Receipts

1. Sales of goods and services	55,000
2. Subsidies	130
3. Interest	6
4. National debt interest	5
5. Dividends	120
6. Income on deposits with the banking system and other financial intermediaries	65
7. Net capital gains	15
8. Consequential loss insurance claims	20
9. Property insurance claims	35
10. Net money capital contributions to unincorporated enterprise and receipts from subscriptions to corporate new issues	345
11. New borrowing:	
(a) Banks	25
(b) Other financial intermediaries	40
12. Redemption and repayments	15
13. Total receipts	55,821

Payments

14. Purchases of goods and services on operating account	47,365
15. Banks and other financial intermediaries. Commission charges for keeping accounts and other services	20
16. Indirect taxes	273
17. Wages and salaries on operating account	3,965
18. Interest on borrowed money	510
19. Contributions to social security funds	30
20. Insurance premiums	76
21. Direct taxes	300
22. Contingency claims to employees and third parties	15
23. Public collective providers	10
24. Dividends and withdrawals	1,580
25. Wages and salaries on capital account	135
26. Purchases of goods and services on capital account	854
27. Net purchases of existing equipment and other assets on capital account	15
28. Redemption and repayment of obligations	20
29. Subscriptions to new issues, etc.	30
30. Net purchase of existing securities	5
31. Total payments	55,203
32. Net increase in money resources	618
	55,821

VI

THE BALANCING STATEMENT

Sector I. Business Enterprises

Balancing statement at close of accounting period

	Aggregated annual accounts		Sector Balance sheet	
Receivables	Dr.	Cr.	Dr.	Cr.
1. Sales of goods and services:				
(i) Debtors at beginning of accounting period for goods delivered or services rendered and invoiced or charged but not paid for during the immediately preceding accounting period, and accrued revenues calculated on a time basis	10,000			
(ii) Sales proceeds		55,000		
(iii) Debtors at close of accounting period for goods delivered or services rendered and invoiced or charged but not paid for during this period, and accrued revenues calculated on a time basis		5,000	5,000	
(iv) Balance carried to the credit of operating account under the classification of 1. Sales 50,000				
2. Subsidies		...	130	
Inventories				
3. Inventories[1] at close of accounting period in respect of unused materials, work in progress or process, and unsold goods. Calculated by reference to opening inventory prices		65	65	
5. (Revised structure)				
10. (Originating structure.) Inventories[1] at beginning of accounting period in respect of unused materials, work in progress or process and unsold goods. Set at the conventional accounting valuation adopted at the close of the immediately preceding accounting period	55			
Payables				
6. (a) Purchases[2] of goods and services:				
(i) Creditors at beginning of accounting period for goods delivered or services rendered and invoiced or charged but not paid for during the immediately preceding accounting period, and accrued expenses calculated on a time basis		8,860		
(ii) Payments for purchases	47,365			
(iii) Creditors at close of accounting period for goods delivered or services rendered and invoiced or charged but not paid for during the immediately preceding accounting period, and accrued expenses calculated on a time basis 4,470				
Say				
Creditors	4,000			4,000
Accrued expenses	470			470
Forward	61,890	69,055	5,065	4,470

[1] Reserve stocks, i.e. commodities bought as a hedge against the future, should be separately identified.

[2] Reserve purchases for stock, i.e. commodities bought as a hedge against the future, should be separately identified.

Payables	Aggregated annual accounts		Sector Balance sheet	
	Dr.	Cr.	Dr.	Cr.
Brought forward	61,890	69,055	5,065	4,470
(iv) Balance carried to the debit of operating account under the classification of 6. Purchases 42,975				
6 (*b*). 1. Banks and other financial intermediaries. Actual commission charges for keeping accounts and other services	20			
6 (*b*). 2. Imputed charges for services	30			
8. (Originating structure)				
7. (Revised structure.) INDIRECT TAXES:				
(i) Provision at beginning of accounting period for unexpired payments in respect of such items as registration licences, local rates, etc. (calculated on a time basis)	37			
(ii) Payments for indirect taxes	273			
(iii) Provision at close of accounting period for unexpired payments (calculated on a time basis)		40	40	
(iv) Balance carried to the debit of operating account under the classification of 7. Indirect taxes 270				
5. (Originating structure)				
8. (Revised structure)				
PAYMENTS TO FACTORS OF PRODUCTION:				
(*a*) Wages, salaries, etc.				
(i) Provision at beginning of accounting period for accrued wages and salaries (calculated on a time basis)		65		
(ii) Payments for wages, salaries, etc.	3,965			
(iii) Provision at close of accounting period for accrued wages and salaries (calculated on a time basis)	75			75
(iv) Balance carried to the debit of operating account under the classification of 8. Payables to factors of production: (*a*) Wages, salaries, etc. 3,975				
5. (Originating structure)				
8. (Revised structure)				
PAYMENTS TO FACTORS OF PRODUCTION:				
(*b*) Interest:				
(i) Provision at beginning of accounting period for accrued interest on borrowed money (calculated on a time basis)		30		
(ii) Payments for interest on borrowed money	510			
(iii) Provision at close of accounting period for accrued interest on borrowed money (calculated on a time basis)	20			20
(iv) Balance carried to the debit of operating account under the classification of 8. Payables to factors of production: (*b*) Interest 500				
9. CONTRIBUTIONS TO SOCIAL SECURITY FUNDS	30			
11. (Originating structure)				
10. (Revised structure)				
DEPRECIATION AND OBSOLESCENCE:				
(i) Arithmetical allocation based on original cost following the accounting convention of the user of a delayed historical cost	300			300
Forward	67,150	69,190	5,105	4,865

	Aggregated annual accounts		Sector Balance sheet	
Payables	*Dr.*	*Cr.*	*Dr.*	*Cr.*
Brought forward	67,150	69,190	5,105	4,865
(ii) Assumed adjustment in a period of rising prices. Management replacement adjustment	140			140
(iii) Balance carried to the debit of operating account under the classification of 10. Depreciation and obsolescence 440				
7. (Originating structure)				
11. (Revised structure):				
(a) INSURANCE PREMIUMS:				
(i) Provision at beginning of accounting period for unexpired premium payments (calculated on a time basis)	5			
(ii) Insurance premium payments	76			
(iii) Provision at close of accounting period for unexpired premium payments (calculated on a time basis)		6	6	
(iv) Balance carried to the debit of operating account under the classification of 11a. Insurance premiums 75				
(b) Imputed charges to policyholders	5			
12. BAD DEBTS	25			25
	67,401			
13. (Originating structure)				
14. (Revised structure)				
OPERATING SURPLUS	1,795			
	69,196	69,196		
Receivables				
15. OPERATING SURPLUS		1,795		
16. (a) INTEREST:				
(i) Provision at beginning of accounting period for accrued interest (calculated on a time basis)	3			
(ii) Interest receipts		6		
(iii) Provision at close of accounting period for accrued interest (calculated on a time basis)		2	2	
(iv) Balance carried to the credit of non-operating account under the classification of 16a. Interest 5				
(b) Transfers from public collective providers: National debt interest		5		
19. (Originating structure)				
17. (Revised structure)				
DIVIDENDS		120		
17. (Originating structure)				
18. (Revised structure)				
INCOME RECEIVABLE (actual) on DEPOSITS with the banking system and other financial intermediaries		65		
17 and 18. (Originating structure)				
19. (Revised structure)				
IMPUTED INCOMES:				
(a) Banking system and other financial intermediaries 30				
(b) Insurance companies and societies 5		35		
Forward	3	2,028	5,113	5,030

	Aggregated annual accounts		Sector Balance sheet	
Receivables	*Dr.*	*Cr.*	*Dr.*	*Cr.*
Brought forward	3	2,028	5,113	5,030
22. (Originating structure)				
21. (Revised structure)				
NET REALISED CAPITAL GAINS available for distribution as income		15		
20. (Originating structure)				
22. (Revised structure)				
CONSEQUENTIAL LOSS INSURANCE CLAIMS		20		
Payables				
25. (Originating structure)				
24. (Revised structure)				
DIRECT TAXES assessable for the current accounting period:	300			
(i) Income tax on profits	×			
(ii) Income tax on the ownership of property	×			
(iii) Income tax on interest and dividends	×			
(iv) Income tax recovered from the dividends included among the payables in the appropriation account	...	×		
(v) Taxes on excess profits	×			
(vi) Balance carried to the debit of non-operating account under the classification of direct taxes assessable for the current accounting period 300				
21. (Originating structure)				
24. (Revised structure)				
(i) Income tax on profits assessable for the current accounting period. As provided in the previous period	...	×		
(ii) Taxes on excess profits over provided in the previous period	...	×		
(iii) Item per originating structure		5		
28. (Originating structure)				
24. (Revised structure)				
Income tax on the profits of the current accounting period assessable in the future period	45			45
26. (Originating structure)				
25. (Revised structure)				
CONTINGENCY CLAIMS to employees and third parties	15			
24. (Originating structure)				
26. (Revised structure)				
PUBLIC COLLECTIVE PROVIDERS. Transfer of operating surplus applicable to publicly controlled enterprises	10			
24. (Originating structure)				
27. (Revised structure)				
CHARITABLE SUBSCRIPTIONS AND DONATIONS	...			
	373			
29. Transfer to appropriation account of surplus	1,695			
	2,068	2,068		
30. Transfer from aggregated profit-and-loss account, non-operating section, of surplus		1,695		
24. (Originating structure)				
31. (Revised structure)				
DIVIDENDS (before deduction of income tax) and WITHDRAWALS				
(i) Proposed dividends (before deduction of income tax) at the beginning of the accounting period		20		
(ii) Dividend payments (before deduction of income tax) and withdrawals	1,580			
Forward	1,580	1,715	5,113	5,075

	Aggregated annual accounts		Sector Balance sheet	
	Dr.	Cr.	Dr.	Cr.
Brought forward	1,580	1,715	5,113	5,075
(iii) Proposed dividends (before deduction of income tax) at the close of the accounting period	30			30
(iv) Balance carried to the debit of appropriation account under the classification of 31. Dividends (before deduction of income tax) and withdrawals 1590				
29. (Originating structure)				
32. (Revised structure) Transfer to reserve of surplus	105			105
	1,715	1,715		
36. (Revised structure) CLOSING INVENTORY adjustment to accord with conventional accounting valuation			5	5
33. (Originating structure) PROPERTY INSURANCE CLAIMS (capital)				35
36. (Originating structure) ASSET FORMATION (capital formation). Payments to factors of production:				
(a) Wages, salaries, etc.			135	
Contributions to social security funds as related to the foregoing wages and salaries			...	
37. (Originating structure) ASSET FORMATION (capital formation). Purchases of goods and services on capital account:				
(i) Creditors at beginning of accounting period				100
(ii) Payments for purchases of goods and services on capital account			854	
(iii) Creditors at close of accounting period			46	
(iv) Asset formation by way of purchases of goods and services 800				
(v) Reciprocal entry for creditors at close of accounting period				46
INDIRECT TAXES associated with capital transactions, e.g. stamp duties on land			...	
DEFERRED CHARGES			...	
38. (Originating structure) ASSET FORMATION (capital formation). Net purchases of existing equipment and other assets on capital account			15	
43. (Originating structure) NET MONEY CAPITAL contributions to unincorporated enterprise and receipts from subscriptions to corporate new issues				345
44. (Originating structure) NEW BORROWING:				
(a) Banks				25
(b) Other financial intermediaries				40
53. (Originating structure) REDEMPTION AND REPAYMENT of obligations			20	
51. (Originating structure) SUBSCRIPTIONS TO NEW ISSUES, etc.			30	
52. (Originating structure) NET PURCHASES OF EXISTING SECURITIES			5	
45. RECEIPTS FROM REDEMPTIONS AND REPAYMENTS				15
50. (Originating structure) Net increase in money resources			618	
Circulating capital fund at beginning of accounting period				1,020
			6,841	6,841

VII

THE SYSTEM OF ACCOUNTS

SOCIAL ACCOUNTS

SECTOR I. PRODUCTIVE ENTERPRISES. BUSINESS ENTERPRISES

(1) Aggregated Profit-and-Loss Account. Operating Section

Payables

Originating structure	Revised structure	Payables			
10	5	Inventories[1] at beginning of accounting period in respect of unused materials, work in progress or process, and unsold goods. Set at the conventional accounting valuation adopted at the close of the immediately preceding accounting period		...	55
6	6 (a)	Purchases of goods[1] and services		42,975	
	(b)	Banks and other financial intermediaries:			
		(1) Actual commission charges for keeping accounts and other services	20		
		(2) Imputed charges for services	30	50	43,025
8	7	Indirect taxes		...	270
5	8	Factors of production:			
		(a) Wages, salaries, etc.		3,975	
		(b) Interest on borrowed money[2] (before deduction of income tax)		500	4,475
9	9	Contributions to social security funds		...	30
11	10	Depreciation and obsolescence:			
		(a) Original cost allocation		300	
		(b) Management replacement adjustment[3]		140	440
7	11	Insurances:			
		(a) Premiums		75	
		(b) Imputed charges to policyholders		5	80
12	12	Allowance for bad debts		...	25
14	13	Total payables			48,400
13	14	Operating surplus		...	1,795
					50,195

Receivables

Originating structure	Revised structure	Receivables		
1	1	Sales of goods and services	...	50,000
2	2	Subsidies	...	130
3	3	Inventories[1] at close of accounting period in respect of unused materials, work in progress or process, and unsold goods. Calculated by reference to opening inventory prices	65	65
		Deduct Inventories at beginning of accounting period per contra	55	
		Measure of inventory formation	10	
4	4	Total receivables		50,195

[NOTE. Since this account was prepared, further research has led to the view that inventory formation is best measured in terms of *end-period* prices. It follows that opening and closing inventories are best shown in this account at *end-period* (or last cost) prices rather than at the opening prices suggested here.]

---

[1] Reserve purchases for stock, i.e. commodities bought as a hedge against the future should be separately identified.

[2] Further research suggests that interest on borrowed money, as a purely financial transaction, should be relegated to the non-operating section of the profit-and-loss account, and replaced here by an interest charge related to the actual net assets employed in the working of enterprises; the corresponding debit to this imputed operating credit would appear in the non-operating section below.

[3] Retained in this account to preserve the economic conception of operating surplus.

(2) Aggregated Profit-and-Loss Account. Non-operating Section

Payables

Originating structure	Revised structure	Payables			
25	24	Direct taxation. Direct taxes assessable for the current accounting period			
		Income tax on profit	×		
		Income tax on the ownership of property	×		
		Income tax on interest and dividends	×	×	
		Less Income tax recovered from the dividends included among the payables in the appropriation account	...	×	
		Taxes on excess profits	...	×	
				300	
21	24	*Deduct* Income tax on profits assessable for the current accounting period as provided in the previous period	...	×	
		Taxes on excess profits over provided in the previous period[1]	...	5	
					295
28	24	Income tax on the profits of the current accounting period assessable in the future period	...	45	
					340
26	25	Contingency claims to employees and third parties	...	15	
24	26	Public collective providers. Transfer of operating surplus applicable to publicly controlled enterprises	...	10	
24	27	Charitable subscriptions and donations	...	...	
	28	Total payables			365
	29	Transfer to appropriation account of surplus	...		1,695
			...		2,060

Receivables

Originating structure	Revised structure	Receivables		
15	15	Operating surplus	...	1,795
16	16(a)	Interest	5	10
	16(b)	Transfers from public collective providers—national debt interest (before deduction of income tax)	5	120
19	17	Dividends (before deduction of income tax)	...	65
17	18	Income receivable (actual) on deposits with the banking system and other financial intermediaries	...	
17 and 18	19	Imputed incomes:		35
		(a) Banking system and other financial intermediaries	30	
		(b) Insurance companies and societies	5	
...	20	Net rents (before deduction of income tax) from property investments	...	...
22	21	Net realised capital gains available for distribution as income	...	15
20	22	Insurance claims in respect of consequential loss and contingency claims to employees and third parties	...	20
	23	Total receivables		2,060

[1] Underprovisions will fall to be dealt with by additions.

(3) Aggregated Appropriation Account

Originating structure	Revised structure			Revised structure		Originating structure
24	30	Dividends (before deduction of income tax) and withdrawals	1,590	30	Transfer from aggregated profit-and-loss account—non-operating section—of surplus	1,695
29	31	Transfer to reserve of surplus	105			
	32		**1,695**			**1,695**

(4) Aggregated Resting Account (Movements in Sector Balance Sheets)

Originating structure	Revised structure				Originating structure	Revised structure			
36	41	Gross fixed asset formation (capital formation): Payments for factors of production—wages and salaries	135				Depreciation and obsolescence:		
	42	Contributions to Social Security Funds as related to wages and salaries	...		32	33	(i) Arithmetical allocation based on original cost following the accounting convention of the user of a delayed historical cost	300	
37	43	Purchases of goods and services	800				(ii) Management replacement adjustment	140	440
	44	Indirect taxes associated with capital transactions, e.g. stamp duties on land	...		33	34	Property insurance claims (capital)	...	35
38	45	Net purchases of existing equipment and other assets on capital account	15	950	42	35	Appropriation account — Transfer to reserve of surplus (retainable income—corporate enterprises saving)	...	105
		Investments:				36	Closing inventory adjustment to accord with conventional accounting valuation	...	5
51	46	Subscriptions to new issues, etc.	30		43	37	Net money capital contributions to unincorporated enterprise and receipts from subscriptions to corporate new issues	...	345
52	47	Net purchases of existing securities	5	35	44	38	New borrowing:		
	48	Deferred charges (other than unexpired payments entering into the assessment of circulating capital)	...	20			(i) Banks	25	
		Redemption and repayment of obligations					(ii) Other financial intermediaries	40	65
		Circulating capital funds:			45	39	Receipts from redemptions and repayments	...	15
53	49	(i) Opening inventories	55		41	40	Deferred liability. Income tax on the profits of the current accounting period assessable in the future period	...	45
	50	(ii) Closing inventories at same prices	65						
		(iii) Inventory formation	10						
		(iv) Closing inventory adjustment to accord with conventional accounting valuation	5	15					
		(v) Opening net debtors	965						
		(vi) Closing net debtors	407						
			-558	-583					
			-25						
50		(vii) Allowance for bad debts							
		(viii) Opening money resources	Nil						
		(ix) Closing money resources	618	618					
				1,055					**1,055**

VIII

AN EXPLANATION OF THE ITEMS IN THE SYSTEM OF ACCOUNTS

SALES

(1) 1. *Sales of Goods and Services*

This item represents the receivable value of all types of goods sold at all stages of processing, *and services* of all kinds rendered during the accounting period. Appropriate adjustments have been made to actual receipts in respect of opening and closing debtors and accrued revenues. The latter have been calculated on a time basis where services are so rendered and paid for. For the purposes of this statement of accounts rent is treated as a service and not as a factor of production. Purchase tax passed on to buyers is included in the sales value of the goods. Discounts, rebates and allowances are deducted in arriving at sales values.

INVENTORIES

(1) 5 *(Revised structure)*; 10 *(Originating structure)*. *Inventories of unused materials, work in progress or process, and unsold goods at beginning of accounting period*

It is intended that this item should be set at the conventional accounting valuation of 'cost or lower market value' as taken in such terms at the close of the immediately preceding accounting period.[1] In this connection, it should be made plain that so far as concerns the inventory statement of unrecovered process costs, the conventional accounting valuation is read as excluding standing costs covering the facilities of production where such costs are related to a continuing enterprise with a relatively large output of units of production.

A modified statement of the operating account, in terms of variable and standing items, would make this clear by limiting inventories to the variable section. Thus:

Modified operating account			
Opening inventories	×	Variable receivables	×
Variable payables	×	Closing inventories	×
Variable margin	×		
	×		×
Standing payables	×	Variable margin	×
Operating margin	×		
	×		×

[1] Since these notes were written, further research has led to the view that inventory formation is best measured in terms of *end-period* prices. It follows that *both* opening and closing inventories are best shown in the operating account at *end-period* (or last cost) prices, but see Appendix II.

It should be observed that standing payables are ordinarily related to standard outputs when it comes to a test of internal efficiency. So-called standard cost accounting procedure sets similar standards for variable payables and ordinarily seeks to measure inventory values on this basis.

A statement of operating accounts in terms of variable and operating margins may be preferred by economists as constituting a first basis for an analysis which might emphasise marginal costs and revenues if applied to a series of short-term accounts.

It is not entirely irrelevant to suggest a practical doubt whether theoretical conceptions of marginal cost entirely correspond with the influences affecting the factor cost situation in the real world. Unit factor costs are not always either severable or independently measurable by progression although they may be calculated from a series of totals abstracted from the possible results of experience. In many businesses additions to output tend to advance more naturally by groups a situation which involves bunches of input costs rather than units. For this reason standard cost accounting technique, which is a practical instrument of control, attempts to concentrate attention on the efficiency of representative and essential processes, under given conditions, for its measurable standards rather than on units of production.

In practice many variable and standing payables are not mutually exclusive, and it is usual for most business enterprises to adopt some conventional differentiation which generally errs on the side of caution by the overstatement of standing charges.

We may add the observation that when it comes to a question of inventory values, raw materials and work in process take on the nature of internal operating transfers, an emphasis which points to conventional methods of valuation for the reason that 'value' is here an internal affair. Unsold finished goods are much more an external affair when it becomes a matter of their value, although accounting theory sticks to a conventional internal valuation in order to secure an accounting notion of profit in terms of *actual realisation on sale*. Although the economic emphasis is on the current market price of the converted goods, accounting theory is concentrated on the time of the carriage of the profit. It is an old accounting maxim that there is no profit until goods have been both produced *and sold*, a maxim which may sometimes disfigure economic assessments of optimum outputs, in terms of production, from accounting documents.

It has been observed that the opening inventories are set at the conventional accounting method of valuation adopted at the close of the immediately preceding accounting period. This method of valuation is experimentally retained here as a practical measure offering a practical advantage, since it is an essential feature of this system of social accounts that it shall fall into line as nearly as may be possible with modern accounting practices and conventions.[1] It is realised, however, that it may involve some statistical difficulties when it comes to a question of correcting for price variations between different accounting periods.

[1] But see note 1 at the foot of page 55.

(1) 3. *Inventories of unused materials, work in progress or process,*
and unsold goods at close of accounting period

In the system of accounts which we are now putting forward it is
proposed that the value statement of this item shall be calculated on the
same pricing basis as was used for the value statement of inventories at
the beginning of the accounting period. Thus if 100 units of classified
stock marked 'A' were taken into the opening inventory at a cost of
£10 per unit then, if 80 units is the quantity on hand at the close of
the accounting period, this will be taken into the closing inventory at
the identical price of £10 per unit, notwithstanding the fact that the
relatively current cost of each of these 80 units may be higher or
lower than £10, or that the alternative 'lower market value' of the
accounting convention may be higher or lower than £10. The intention
of this standardisation of the closing inventory valuation is to emphasise
quantity changes.[1]

The procedure we have adopted will involve a closing adjustment
to bring this relatively standard closing valuation into line with the
conventional accounting valuation which will be carried into actual
business accounts. In a period of rising prices this adjustment should be
positive and in a period of falling prices, negative. In the operating
section of the aggregated profit-and-loss account the refinement of
showing opening and closing inventory items as inset set-offs, has been
introduced to throw up a measure of positive or negative inventory
formation.

Accountants will notice a departure from accounting practice in the
positioning of the closing inventory adjustment. Here it appears as
a direct entry in the resting account. The purpose of this divergent
treatment is to keep the inventory adjustment out of saving with a view
to safeguarding the ultimate conception of saving as equivalent to asset
formation plus net lending abroad.

Although we have temporarily adopted the standardisation of inventory
valuations at opening prices we are aware of the practical difficulties
which accountants are likely to experience in giving effect to this sugges-
tion, particularly when it comes to the matter of work in progress.[2] Quite
apart from this we know that there are cases, peculiarly relevant to
merchanting enterprises, where there is a marked change in the nature

[1] As a matter of strict theory it would seem that the valuations of the opening and
closing inventories should be standardised on the basis of average costs, calculated as
the mean between the *costs* entering into the opening valuation and the *costs* entering
into the closing valuation. In this way it would be possible to reveal a measure of
inventory profit in line with the concept of economists. From the technical accounting
standpoint such a standardisation of valuations would involve twofold adjustments in
relation to the conventional accounting valuations adopted for opening and closing
inventories in the ordinary course of business practice. On this question, however,
see the later developments referred to in note 1 at the foot of page 55, and in
Appendix II.

[2] This equally applies to a standardisation at *end-period* prices.

of the goods carried in stock at the start and finish of an accounting period. Nevertheless, we feel that some disclosure on the lines we have put forward might be attempted even though it may require a degree of estimation and judgment. One course might be to select a number of representative items for the purpose of constructing a general index of the price rise or fall as between the opening and closing dates. We recognise that the standardisation of inventories may involve some distortion where there are large changes in stocks held for speculative purposes. Later we may seek to isolate this difficulty by working from the conception of a normal operating inventory for a prescribed level of output, a conception which has something in common with the accounting notion of a base stock.

There is also an obvious problem associated with the alternative of cost or lower market value in the conventional methods of inventory valuation commonly adopted in business accounts. In this connection it might be an advantage if accountants could be persuaded to show the cost valuation and disclose its basis, with a separate disclosure of the adjustment to lower market values.

PURCHASES

(1) 6 (a) (Revised structure); 6 (Originating structure).
Purchases of goods and services

This item represents the payable value of all types of goods purchased and services rendered. It is a wide classification which includes purchases of raw materials, semi-finished and finished products. It takes in services of all kinds including professional charges and fees to public authorities for actual services rendered. It excludes payables classified for the purposes of these accounts as made to factors of production, but *rent is included* as a service. Insurance premiums and indirect taxes are excluded and appear as separate items in the operating section of the aggregated profit-and-loss account.

Appropriate adjustments have been made to actual payments in respect of opening and closing creditors and accrued expenses. The latter have been calculated on a time basis where services are so rendered and paid for. It will be clear to accountants that an item for unexpired payments, calculated on a time basis, might very well have been taken into this classification, but in the interests of statement simplicity, it has been limited to the separate caption for insurance premiums and to the items for registration licences and local rates included in indirect taxes, on the grounds that these offer the most common forms of unexpired payments.

In terms of accounting profit statements classified according to primary data, amounts included under the following headings will fall to be brought within the social accounting designation of purchases of goods and services.

All forms of purchases (e.g. materials).
Consumable tools.
Fuel.
Intermediate goods and sub-contracts.
Printing and stationery.
All forms of services.
Repairs and maintenance.

Power.	Telephones.
Lighting.	Telegrams.
Heating.	Cables.
Water.	Carriage.
Postages.	Travelling.

Advertising for current benefits.
Business subscriptions.
Professional charges for current benefits.

Laundry.	Rent.

Royalties (at their gross equivalents before deduction of income tax).[1]
All forms of hire charges.
Accounting Losses on Exchange in so far as they are directly attributable to the purchases of goods and services.
And so on.

Accountants will find that practically all kinds of purchases of goods and services to be debited in profit-and-loss accounts can be fitted into one or other of this type of primary accounting classification.

Discounts, rebates and allowances are treated as direct deductions in arriving at purchase values.

It is usual in actual business accounts to include the purchase of reserve stocks—commodities bought as a hedge against the future—either in one or other of the headings for purchases or as a separately classified debit in the profit-and-loss account. In so far as such stocks do not constitute an element in current operations they are ordinarily carried into the closing inventory where they virtually make their way to capital account. For the purposes of social accounting it is highly desirable that such reserve purchases and stocks should be separately identified in the purchases and inventory classifications appearing in the operating section of the aggregated profit-and-loss account. Alternatively the purchase of reserve stocks might temporarily appear as a direct capital purchase.

---

[1] It should be noticed that on 13 March 1943 the Institute of Chartered Accountants in England and Wales recommended that 'Annual charges for debenture and other interest, *royalties and similar annual payments* should be charged gross' in the profit-and-loss accounts of companies. *Recommendations on Accounting Principles of the Institute of Chartered Accountants in England and Wales* to its members on certain aspects of the accounts of companies engaged in industrial and commercial enterprises, IV (2), 36, p. 11 (Gee and Company (Publishers), Ltd.). See our comments on the classification: 'Payables to factors of production (*b*) Interest.'

6 (*b*) 1. *Bank charges. Bank and other financial intermediaries. Actual
commission charges for keeping accounts and other services.*

It will be appreciated that these charges are dealt with on a payable
basis, but for the sake of simplicity in stating the system the opening
and closing creditors are here assumed to be zero.

In business accounts accruals for actual bank commission charges are
commonly ignored provided that a full annual charge appears to the
debit of the yearly profit-and-loss account.

6 (*b*) 2. *Banks and other financial intermediaries. Imputed
charges for services*

This is an item which at once raises difficulties for accountants and
it is doubtful if those responsible for the preparation of business enterprise accounts can ever really estimate it with any show of accuracy.
In the operating account of primary transactions of the individual unit
it is probably better not to attempt any such measurement, leaving it
to be dealt with by a conventional interpolation to be set in the
aggregated social accounts by those responsible for the aggregation.

By way of an explanation of the sense in which this charge is imputed,
most accountants will be familiar with the case in which, because of the
size of the current account balances carried, a bank makes *no* commission
charge for keeping the account, or if a commission charge is made it is
inadequate to cover the actual banking services rendered. Or again,
a similar situation may arise because of the size of the overdraft or loan
account carried. It is therefore argued, from the standpoint of social
accounting, that in so far as banks do not charge sufficient to cover the
value of the services they render, the 'interest' payments to banks must
include a part service charge and are not, therefore, true interest in the
sense required of a factor share. The imputed charge is an attempt to
measure this service charge in order to safeguard the generation of
income in the banking sector of the national economy, as otherwise we
reach the strange position of the banking system contributing nothing
to the national income.

The social accounting convention for the assessment of imputed bank
charges assumes an income 'imputed to bank depositors for the use of
their money equal to the excess of interest and dividends received by
banks over interest paid out and this income is assumed to be used in
"paying" for uncharged banking services'.

The effect of this social accounting interpolation is to carry into the
non-operating section of the aggregated profit-and-loss account of
business enterprises a conventional income based on that excess of
interest *and dividends* receivable by banks over interest payable which is
imputed to business enterprises with a corresponding imputed payable
for uncharged banking services in the operating section.

As we have said, business enterprises cannot be expected to estimate on their own account imputed bank service charges. To say the least of it, the accuracy of any such imputation for particular undertakings would be more than doubtful. But what accountants will tend to argue is that in those cases which are relevant they already record a composite debit under the style of Bank Interest which in point of fact comprises both the factor interest and the service charge. They will suggest that they have covered both sets of payables under the one heading and that in the aggregated system imputation should only be resorted to in order to reveal that analysis, and to provide a payable which properly makes its way into the operating receivables of the banking sector.

It seems that such an argument will depend upon the validity of its underlying assumption that interest on business enterprise advances covers the cost of all services to business enterprise customers. But in so far as monies deposited with banks are not advanced to customers, but are, in fact, invested in securities, it may be that the resulting dividend income is contributing to the costs of the services rendered to customers, in which case there seems nothing for it but to accept the social accounting convention referred to at the beginning of this particular discussion. If we do take this line we must recognise that it involves a partial duplication in the operating section of the aggregated profit-and-loss account of business enterprises, and to that extent the *operating surplus* of this sector will be understated, though in point of fact this understatement is immediately recovered in the *non-operating* section through the conventional receivable. Accountants will question this treatment on the grounds that it does not square with their conception of operating profit.

For all practical purposes it is the part service charge included in the actual bank interest paid which is the measure of the duplication, and assuming it to be ascertainable, this amount would need to be deducted from the full imputed charge. The conventional non-operating income credit would require a corresponding deduction of equivalent amount.

Throughout this discussion it will be apparent that in the banking sector the conception of an imputed service charge with its corresponding imputation of income to whoever is responsible for the payable, requires analysis as between business enterprises and persons. At first sight one would think that such an analysis would necessitate some kind of apportionment of the dividend income contributing to the cost of services to business enterprises and the cost of services to persons. Yet it does not seem that it would be valid to base the destination of the imputations on a strict analysis between business enterprises and persons of each debit and credit banking item entering into the assessment of the imputations. In fact, the cost of services to persons might be quite out of proportion to the interest received from persons, and so on with each actual item entering into the assessment of the imputation. It seems that what has to be done is to regard the total of all interest and dividends received less all interest paid as equivalent to the costs of all services rendered, and then to attempt the application of some form of cost accounting to arrive at the division between business enterprises and persons, a process which may give rise to some rather arbitrary assumptions.

INDIRECT TAXES

(1) 8 *(Originating structure)*; 7 *(Revised structure)*

This heading takes in all indirect taxes, assessed on or attachable to goods and services, which are charged as expenses in the operating profit-and-loss accounts of business enterprises. Examples of such taxes are customs and excise duties, purchase tax, local rates, motor registration dues, business licence duties, certain stamp duties, and Government agency registration and audit fees.

As with the case of other operating expenses adjustment to actual payments in respect of opening and closing creditors may be necessary to arrive at the payables relevant to the accounting period. Such items as local rates and registration licences are usually paid in advance for a stated time period. Accordingly, at the accounting date the unexpired portion of the payment (calculated on a time basis) is carried over to the next period, and as a matter of accounting technique is dealt with in much the same way as a debtor.

PAYABLES TO FACTORS OF PRODUCTION

(1) 5 *(Originating structure)*; 8 *(Revised structure)*

(a) Wages, Salaries, etc.

This classification covers all payments made by business enterprises for wages and salaries, and appropriate adjustments are carried in to provide for the opening and closing accruals (calculated on a time basis) with the intention of portraying the actual expenditure of the relevant accounting period. It should not be overlooked that some firms adopt the course of paying monthly salaries in advance, a practice which may very well necessitate provisions for unexpired payments (calculated on a time basis) at the beginning and end of the accounting period. In the interests of simplicity this type of adjustment has been omitted from wages and salaries in the accounts which accompany this text. Examples of such provisions are to be found under indirect tax payments and insurance premium payments.

'Wages and salaries' is a heading which should include the payable value of income in kind, e.g. free board and lodging, free coal given to miners, and employers' contributions to *private* pension schemes. In point of fact it would be an advantage if such issues in kind were disclosed separately. All net benefits to employees should be dealt with as part of their income. Nevertheless, it should be clearly understood that such income does not include the expenses of earning it in any specific trade. Thus, if workmen are required to purchase tools or *working* clothing out of their earnings the amounts so payable by the workmen should be excluded from wages and salaries, and included under the heading of purchases of goods and services. Individual firms should be reasonably acquainted with the circumstances of employment in their particular trade and should not find it too difficult to make a monetary imputation which covers this transfer.

It sometimes happens that an employee is allowed the use of a business car for private purposes. Where the whole cost of user is charged direct in the business accounts, that part of the cost which is imputed to private purposes should be brought in with wages and salaries. In the assessment of all such *internal* adjustments it is important to be consistent.

(b) Interest

In this context interest is related to all those forms of borrowed money which do not confer proprietorship rights,[1] e.g. debentures in contra-distinction to ordinary shares. Appropriate opening and closing adjustments to payments are made in respect of accruals (calculated on a time basis) to give the amounts payable in the accounting period. Payments of interest made in advance of the time period they are intended to cover may be encountered,[1] in which case it will be necessary to provide for opening and closing adjustments in respect of the parts of those payments calculated (on a time basis) as unexpired at the accounting dates.

In March 1943 the Institute of Chartered Accountants in England and Wales issued a recommendation on accounting principles[2] which made the comment that income tax deducted from payments of debenture and other interest was in effect assessed on a company for collection from the payee. Therefore, it was recommended that annual charges for debenture and other interest should be charged gross in the profit-and-loss accounts of companies. Social accounting requires a similar treatment since it is essentially concerned with the income generated in each sector of the economy. Thus, the enterprise making the interest payment will virtually dispose of the income tax held back, by *contra* entry when the time comes for the payment of direct taxes on profits. Technically, this is achieved by the disallowance of interest as a charge against the profits assessed for income tax purposes. In the social accounts which record the receivable destination of the interest, the gross equivalent will be shown as the receivable and the income tax deduction will appear as a payable for direct taxes. We may notice that this is a portrayal which falls into line with another recommendation of

[1] Discounts on bills of exchange in so far as they constitute payments for the use of money may be taken as included under this classification.
[2] *Recommendations on Accounting Principles of the Institute of Chartered Accountants in England and Wales*, IV (2), p. 11 (Gee and Company (Publishers) Ltd.).

the Institute of Chartered Accountants who, when dealing with the treatment of taxation in company accounts,[1] recommended that 'income tax on revenue taxed before receipt should be included as part of the taxation charge for the year and the relative income should be brought to credit gross'.

(1) 9. EMPLOYERS' CONTRIBUTIONS TO SOCIAL SECURITY FUNDS

This heading calls for little comment. Employers' contributions to social security funds are dealt with in the accompanying accounts in the same way as indirect taxes. In business accounts it is an item which is commonly described either as national insurance or as national health, pensions and unemployment insurance. It is obviously an entry which is always present in any account which includes payables to factors of production for wages and salaries.

DEPRECIATION AND OBSOLESCENCE

(1) 11 (*Originating structure*); 10 (*Revised structure*)

Provision for depreciation and obsolescence is one of the most contentious items in business accounts when it comes to questions of profit measurement. The economic conception of such a provision requires the building up of a fund which will conserve circulating resources sufficient to enable equipment to be replaced by the time it is worn out or obsolete, thereby reinstating the facilities of production.

Economists have implied that in a system of private enterprise the duty of looking after the community's capital equipment rests with the private people who own the capital. Thus, the preservation of capital equipment is an obligation which follows proprietorship and in the circumstances of the modern industrial structure it may be supposed that this duty is delegated to managements. With some show of reason one writer has remarked that 'if capital is used to better advantage as a result of private ownership, and if the profits which are received by the owners are on the whole not more than a reasonable return for the care which they take of their property, then it may be more to the interest of the whole community (including those who are not owners of property) to have capital administered by owners rather than by public officials (who would also require to be paid). But it is only possible to make out a good case for private ownership along these lines, if the owners of property do actually look after the capital goods which they own; in practice it has become less and less true that they do so.'[2] However much we may feel impelled to question the last comment we cannot fail to concede the foundation necessity to keep up so-called real capital as

---

[1] *Recommendations on Accounting Principles. of the Institute of Chartered Accountants in England and Wales*, III (2) (*d*), p. 10.

[2] *The Social Framework*, by J. R. Hicks, p. 84 (Oxford: Clarendon Press, 1942).

soon as we press the problem beyond the level of proprietorship interests to the standpoint of society, and this is the concept sought here.

Accountants, the people most intimately concerned with the structure of business accounts, have so far had little or no occasion to look beyond proprietorship interests. Within the limits of the short-term pressure of expediency it has been their duty to portray a reasonable view of the affairs of an enterprise to its proprietors. They have, therefore, looked upon the matter in terms of the protection of contributed money capital, and quite naturally this view has coincided with the requirements of the legal framework within which they have been called upon to function. Thus, to the accounting mind: 'Depreciation represents that part of the cost of a fixed asset to its owner which is not recoverable when the asset is finally put out of use by him.'[1] The accountant recognises three factors in the assessment of depreciation when considered in relation to the background we have discussed, viz.:

the cost of the asset, which is known, the probable value realisable on ultimate disposal, which can generally be estimated only within fairly wide limits, and the length of time during which the asset will be commercially useful to the undertaking. In most cases, this last factor is not susceptible of precise calculation. Provisions for depreciation are therefore in most cases matters of estimation, based upon the available experience and knowledge, rather than of accurate determination. They require adjustment from time to time in the light of changes in experience and knowledge, including prolongation of useful life due to exceptional maintenance expenditure, curtailment due to excessive use, or obsolescence not allowed for in the original estimate of the commercially useful life of the asset.

There are several methods of apportioning depreciation as between the several financial periods which constitute the anticipated useful life of the asset. Those most commonly employed in industrial and commercial concerns in this country are the straight-line method and the reducing balance method.

Subject to any periodic adjustment which may be necessary, the straight-line method (computed by providing each year a fixed proportion of the cost of the asset) spreads the provision equally over the period of anticipated use. It is used almost universally in the United States of America and Canada and to a large extent in this country. Though other methods may be appropriate in the case of some classes of assets, the balance of informed opinion now favours the straight-line method as being the most suitable for general application.[2]

And so accounting technique provides for depreciation of fixed assets in the operating accounts of business enterprise by methods which resort to simple arithmetical allocations of delayed costs over the periods of anticipated use. But this is not to say that accountants are unaware of the deeper problem, for in Section IX of the *Recommendations on Accounting*

[1] *Recommendations on Accounting Principles of the Institute of Chartered Accountants in England and Wales*, IX, 'Depreciation of Fixed Assets', p. 24 (i) (Gee and Company (Publishers) Ltd.).

[2] *Ibid.* p. 24 (i), (ii).

Principles of the Institute of Chartered Accountants at line 106 (p. 24 (v))
we meet belated but highly significant comments to the effect that:
'amounts set aside out of profits for obsolescence which cannot be
foreseen, or for a possible increase in the cost of replacement are matters
of financial prudence. Neither can be estimated with any degree of
accuracy. They are in the nature of reserves and should be treated as
such in the accounts.' Here we are brought face to face with the crux
of the matter. In its first definition of operating profit accounting
technique is very largely preoccupied with historical costs and historical
revenues for the very good reason that these constitute the originating
data for its summary formulations. Costs used up in the course of
operations must be provided for. If it is thought that the recovery of the
original cost of a fixed asset is insufficient to meet its replacement cost
then the deficiency cover is a matter for management policy in the way
of financial prudence and when brought into business accounts it should
be treated as a reserve. It is known that the directors of some companies
do make estimates of the replacement costs of fixed assets and where
these have risen in relation to original costs they take care to retain
profits sufficient to cover the difference; though this retention is seldom
disclosed as part of a replacement fund it usually resides in one or other
of the company's free revenue reserves. There we have the accountancy
view of the situation.

Social accounting is concerned to face the *real* issues and as a consequence places the emphasis on the adequacy of depreciation or
replacement funds rather than on the using up of delayed historical costs.
The applied economic investigator encounters difficulties as soon as he
begins to look at the ordinary run of business accounts, for he is hard put
to it to find a real measure of the replacement of fixed equipment, and
these difficulties are not lessened by the tendency of some undertakings
to write down certain of their fixed assets to nominal sums at the earliest
possible moment in order to convey an impression of financial strength.
His aggregations fail unless he is presented with business accounts in
which some attempt is made to estimate and disclose the real measure
of the funds required to replace the fixed assets used up in the course of
operations.

At the beginning of this note we said that depreciation provisions
should be calculated for the purposes of social accounts in such a way
that in due course they would provide a sum which would reinstate the
asset at the close of its useful life. Such provisions are intended to take
account not only of price changes, but also of changes in the design of
equipment. The purpose is to provide funds at the end of the life of the
equipment to purchase fresh equipment which in some sense may be
regarded as equivalent. Underlying the whole question of provisions
for depreciation is the fundamental assumption that the proper costs of
repair and maintenance of the equipment will be charged to operating
account and in the system of social accounts here put forward such costs
will show under the classification of payables to factors of production for

wages and salaries, and under the heading 'purchases of goods and services'.

As we have seen, accounting technique on the subject of depreciation as applied to business accounts safeguards the ability of an enterprise to end up with enough funds to repay its money capital. If the prices of fixed assets are rising it is sometimes argued that this will imply that in the new period an enterprise is faced with the alternative of either curtailing its operations or adding to its borrowing if it is to maintain the same level of output, and that this is evidence that an insufficient amount was set aside to depreciation or replacement fund in the first period. This would be true if it were not for the fact that in practice firms conserve their resources by retaining profits either in the form of unappropriated surplus or general reserves. But from the standpoint of social accounting this obscures the measure of saving and results in a somewhat ambiguous portrayal of both depreciation or replacement funds, and saving.

If by chance equipment should actually cost less to replace than it originally cost, it cannot be overlooked that the money capital of the enterprise must still be covered so far as concerns eventual repayment though it is clear that operations on the same scale as heretofore can now be carried on with less new borrowing than before. Thus, it may be said that in maintaining its money capital a firm safeguards its ability to repay its money indebtedness, although without a sufficient accumulation of savings it may not be able to continue its scale of operations in the next period without increased borrowing. On the other hand if *real* capital has been maintained in circumstances of rising prices a firm is assured of sufficient resources both to repay its indebtedness and to install equivalent new equipment without increasing either its contributed capital or its borrowing. In our aggregated system of social accounts the repayment of money indebtedness is nothing more than an internal affair, but ability to replace equipment is of fundamental importance.

From the standpoint of the individual enterprise depletion allowances may be dealt with by making provisions sufficient to compensate for the gradual using up of wasting natural assets so as to enable assets of equivalent value to be purchased when the existing ones are exhausted. In the memorandum accompanying the originating system of social accounts[1] it has been pointed out that 'for an individual enterprise this will be a positive sum of money, but for the community as a whole it will be zero, since we are considering the free gifts of nature and not the equipment or improvements needed to exploit them'. It might here be observed that there are both legal and accounting precedents for the view that no depletion allowances need be provided on the grounds that in the circumstances of the exploitation of a natural wasting asset distributions to proprietors by way of dividend constitute in part

[1] Op. cit.

a repayment of the original money capital contributed to the exploitation venture.[1]

It has been urged that differing accounting conventions applied to the question of provisions for depreciation lead to incomparability when it comes to the purposes of social accounting, although over the long period this may not be so important as might be imagined. Thus, there are some cases in which firms work on a replacement rather than a depreciation basis. Under this method the cost of actual renewals and replacements are charged to the operating section of the profit-and-loss account as and when they are made, and no provisions for such replacements are set aside in advance. Providing that such replacements are conveniently and fairly evenly spread over a long period, as is probably the case with an old-established enterprise, and that they are easily covered out of current operating profits, no real harm is done, and on the whole the method will approximate to the concept sought here.

We should add one last comment which was made in the memorandum which accompanied the originating structure of social accounts:[2]

In certain cases no allowances for depreciation or renewal are made at all. This is true for example in the case of local authority common services in the United Kingdom. What is done in these cases is to charge loan repayments and payments to sinking fund for future discharge of debt against operating expenses on such a basis that there is a reasonable correspondence between the life of the assets and the period over which the borrowing used to finance them is repaid. These sums may be treated as deductions from gross capital formation in lieu of depreciation allowances, although it will be observed that they maintain only money capital intact.

We have mentioned that accounting statements of operating profit are drawn with a fairly firm emphasis on historical costs and historical revenues. If, therefore, business men and their accountants could be persuaded to disclose replacement adjustments to original cost depreciation allocations in business accounts, it seems clear that in order to preserve accounting notions of profit on a dependable basis such adjustments would fall to be dealt with in the second section of the financial accounting document known as the profit-and-loss account. In November 1945 the Research Committee of the Society of Incorporated Accountants published a memorandum in which the point was made that a strict accounting view would incline to a first statement of income in terms of realised profit in cash or its equivalent. It then

---

[1] Thus, No. IX 2 (d) of the *Recommendations on Accounting Principles of the Institute of Chartered Accountants*, dealing with Mines, Oil Wells, Quarries and similar assets of a wasting character which are consumed in the form of basic raw material or where the output is sold as such, states: 'Provision for depreciation and depletion should be made according to the estimated exhaustion of the asset concerned. In the case of an undertaking formed for the purpose of exploiting this particular class of asset, if the practice is to make no provision this should be made clear in the accounts so that shareholders may realise that dividends are, in part, a return of capital' (12 January 1945, p. 24 (v); Gee and Company (Publishers), Ltd.).

[2] Op. cit.

recommended the setting up of an adjustment statement (i.e. ordinarily the second section of the profit-and-loss account) to show so-called *policy* reserves.[1]

In this context the main concern of economists is that there should be this kind of disclosure in business accounts. Social accounting is concerned to arrive at the true aggregated operating surplus, and it is for this reason that the replacement adjustment to original cost depreciation allowances has been shown in the accompanying accounts as an integral item in the operating section of the aggregated profit-and-loss account rather than find inclusion in the non-operating section.

INSURANCE PREMIUMS AND IMPUTED CHARGES TO POLICYHOLDERS

(1) 7 (*Originating structure*); 11 (*a*) and (*b*) (*Revised structure*)

The nature of the payables directly included as insurance premiums is very largely that of provision for contingencies. There is, however, a relatively small proportion which is properly related to the purchase of services in so far as it may be taken to cover the operating expenses and profits of the insurance companies. It is customary to pay insurance premiums in advance of the period of indemnity and, as we have observed elsewhere in this context, to arrive at the equivalent payable charges of the accounting period it is necessary to make adjustments to actual premium payments for the unexpired proportions (calculated on a time basis) at the opening and closing accounting dates. This is what has been done in the accompanying system of accounts.

It will be noticed that at (*b*) of this classification charges are imputed to policyholders. This imputation is not unlike that which we have already considered in the case of bank charges, and much the same difficulties present themselves. It is an imputation which cannot readily be made by the draftsman of the accounts of the individual enterprise, and ordinarily it must be left to the social accounting aggregator. In the system we are discussing this imputation is made to cover the circumstance that part of the receivables of insurance companies answering the redistribution of resources in respect of contingency claims, and the costs and profits peculiar to the conduct of such services, arises from investment income. In order to attain a measure of the real charge to business enterprises, an imputation is made equivalent to the investment income of insurance companies and societies allocated to business enterprise business, and this imputation appears as a payable in the operating account of Sector 1, to be recovered as non-operating income imputed as receivable from the insurance companies and societies in the non-operating section of the aggregated profit-and-loss account.

---

[1] 'The Measurement of Profits. The approach of the Accountant and the approach of the Economist contrasted—The Incorporated Accountants' Research Committee', *Accountancy*, November 1945.

(1) 12. Bad Debts

In the social accounting aggregation of business accounts the term 'bad debts' covers a net item. It will be apparent that the bad debts of any one enterprise may have arisen in both its trading relations with other enterprises and with final consumers in person. In so far as they arise with other business enterprises they constitute a negative entry under this classification in the accounts of the destination enterprises. On aggregation, therefore, bad debts between business enterprises will fall out, leaving only those debtor transactions with other sectors of the economy which business enterprise has had to regard as bad. Of these by far the most important is the final consumer in the shape of persons.

The accounting process of writing off debts involves a downward adjustment to a former asset for debtors which is tantamount to a reduction in the circulating capital fund of the enterprise. Since movements of debtors and creditors, in fact all sector balance sheet items, must find their way into the resting account, the writing off of debts necessitates an entry in the resting account.

The social accounting conception of bad debts is that of a periodical chargeable allowance based on experience, and which is therefore ordinarily taken up. As an operating expense it is an allowance which should be based on a strict review of debtors at the accounting date.

Operating Surplus

(1) 13 and 15 (*Originating structure*); 14 and 15 (*Revised structure*)

This is the balancing item in the operating section of the aggregated profit-and-loss account, which is thereafter transferred to the non-operating section of the same account. It is the margin between the operating receivables and payables and is intended to constitute a measure of the aggregated profits of business enterprise directly attributable to the operations of the accounting period. It clearly excludes all forms of income not directly related to the business processes in which the individual enterprises are engaged, e.g. investment income, and it also excludes capital gains. It is obvious that all the items stated in the non-operating account are regarded as arising outside the operating activities of business enterprise and as such are excluded from the assessment of operating surplus.

At this point it should be observed that where enterprises are engaged in subsidiary economic activities, e.g. the letting of properties, these should be the subject of separate operating accounts, the resulting surpluses to be transferred to the aggregated account for income from sources external to the main operations.

(2) 16. INTEREST RECEIVABLE

The receivable for interest is one of the items comprising investment income and for this reason finds its place in the non-operating section of the aggregated profit-and-loss account. It constitutes the interest on security holdings and other outside investments of an enterprise. As was pointed out in the originating memorandum: 'these receipts may come from either the operating or appropriation accounts of other enterprises of all kinds, from public authorities or from the rest of the world.'

In the accompanying system of accounts national debt interest has been separately featured as a transfer from public collective providers, and as such it may be argued that the reciprocal entries of business enterprise receipt and public collective provider payment are sufficient. As a matter of accounting practice it is not usual to accrue national debt interest in business accounts. Nevertheless, if it should happen that the accounts of public collective providers are completely set on a receivable payable basis in the context of social accounting, then it will require that business enterprises shall follow suit if the sector accounts are to be kept self-balancing and reciprocal.

As we have commented elsewhere in the text, current business accounting practice is now very largely in accord with the social accounting principle which states the interest item before deduction of income tax. Much the same comments apply to the dividends credited in the non-operating account as we have made here in relation to interest.

INCOME ON DEPOSITS

17 (*Originating structure*); (2) 18 (*Revised structure*)

This credit to the non-operating account constitutes the actual receivable income on deposits with the banking system and other financial intermediaries. It is commonly described in business accounts under some such caption as 'Bank deposit interest'. Since it is received by business enterprise without deduction of income tax it is a source of income which is liable to direct taxation by direct assessment.

REALISED CAPITAL GAINS

22 (*Originating structure*); (2) 21 (*Revised structure*)

The realised capital gains which are here credited to the non-operating section of the aggregated profit-and-loss account are those which are regarded by business enterprises as available for distribution as income. The accounting view of the matter rests upon certain legal decisions and may be briefly summed up in the statement that a profit on the realisation of any one particular asset cannot be treated as available for distribution as income unless due regard has been paid to the results shown by the accounts of the enterprise as a whole. The significant case which supports this view is that of Foster *v.* New Trinidad Lake Asphalte

Co. Ltd. (1901) 1 Ch. 208. On its formation the company had taken over a number of assets amongst which was a debt which had been dealt with as being of no real value. It subsequently turned out that this debt realised a substantial sum of money, which sum it sought to treat as a capital profit available for distribution as dividend. During the course of the judgment it was said:

> I must not, however, be understood as determining that this sum or a portion of it may not properly be brought into Profit and Loss Account in ascertaining the amount available for dividend. That appears to me to depend upon the result of the whole account for the year. It is clear, I think, that an appreciation in total value of capital assets, if duly realised by sale or getting in of some portion of such assets, may, in a proper case, be treated as available for purposes of dividend.

Thus, it was held that the sum in question could not be distributed as dividend without having regard to the results shown by the accounts as a whole. As Mr de Paula puts the matter: 'Capital profits are available for distribution as dividend, provided that they are realised profits, and that in arriving at the amount available, all charges and losses, both capital and revenue, for the period are brought into account.'[1]

As a matter of financial good sense it is common to find that currently realised capital losses are treated as charges on income in business accounts. Nevertheless, it should be remarked that there is a guiding legal precedent which distinguishes between losses of fixed capital and losses of circulating capital.[2] Circulating capital must be kept up, but when it comes to losses of fixed capital it seems that if either the constitution of an incorporated enterprise or one of its contracts provides that its money capital shall be kept intact before distributable profits are available, then such an enterprise is bound to charge its fixed capital losses against income, but if there are no such limiting conditions then it is not illegal to ignore fixed capital losses when it comes to a question of assessing income available for distribution by way of dividend.

It will be appreciated that movements in asset accounts during an accounting period will ordinarily pass through the resting account. Where realised capital gains are not treated as available income they will remain where they fall in the resting account. If they are regarded as income available for distribution they will pass on to the non-operating section of the aggregated profit-and-loss account.

[1] *The Principles of Auditing*, by F. R. M. de Paula (10th ed.), p. 213.
[2] Verner *v.* General and Commercial Investment Trust (1912), 106 L.T. 49. The expressions 'fixed' and 'circulating' capital have been retained here because they were the expressions used in this case. In accounting terminology fixed and circulating assets would be the better figures.

INSURANCE CLAIMS IN RESPECT OF CONSEQUENTIAL LOSS AND
CONTINGENCY CLAIMS TO EMPLOYEES AND THIRD PARTIES

20 (*Originating structure*); (2) 22 (*Revised structure*)

PROPERTY INSURANCE CLAIMS (CAPITAL)

33 (*Originating structure*); (4) 34 (*Revised structure*)

The first of these items appears as a credit in the non-operating income account while the latter shows as a capital credit in the resting account. This is a treatment consistent with the principles followed in the construction of business accounts. The amounts received in respect of property insurance claims ordinarily relate to the loss of fixed assets, and the proceeds of the claims are used to reinstate these assets. Accordingly, the amount of these claims appears as a negative item to be set against gross asset formation and as such it is shown in the sector balance sheets.

The amounts received in respect of contingency claims to employees and third parties are met by corresponding payments in the non-operating section of the aggregated profit-and-loss account. The intention of consequential loss insurance, however, is to enable an enterprise which has suffered a period of inactivity following some disaster such as a fire to recover at least its standing expenses. Put in another way it may be said that by such insurance the management of an enterprise hope to prevent the period of inactivity or under-activity which normally follows a disaster from adversely affecting the income of the enterprise. Hence amounts received under these types of claim are brought to the credit of the non-operating section of the profit-and-loss account as income recoveries.

DIRECT TAXATION

21, 25, 28 (*Originating structure*); (2) 24 (*Revised structure*)

On 13 March 1943 the Institute of Chartered Accountants in England and Wales issued a series of recommendations dealing with the treatment of direct taxation in the accounts of companies engaged in industrial and commercial enterprises.[1] These recommendations present the accountancy view of provisions for direct taxation and their disclosure in company accounts, and since they are much in line with the treatment sought in social accounts it may not come amiss to make the following direct quotations:

The assessment of liability to national defence contribution and excess profits tax is based on the profits of the accounting period under review. The assessment of liability to income tax is, however, for the fiscal year ending

---

[1] *Recommendations on Accounting Principles of the Institute of Chartered Accountants in England and Wales*, III. 'The treatment of taxation in accounts', pp. 8–10 (Gee and Company (Publishers), Ltd.).

5th April and is normally based on the profits of a preceding accounting period. The minimum or legal amount to be provided for taxation is thus the aggregate of taxes assessable on these bases, apportioned, as regards income tax, according to the period covered by the accounts under review [p. 9, par. 21].

Income tax so apportioned takes no account, however, either of the balance of the liability assessable for the current fiscal year, or of the liability which, in normal circumstances, will arise in respect of profits included in the accounts but not assessable until the following fiscal year. Further, unless provision be made year by year for income tax based on each year's results, the trend of net available profits will not be apparent, and cases will arise where the profits earned in a succeeding period will bear a disproportionate charge for taxation—indeed, they may even be insufficient to meet it [p. 9, par. 22].

It is recommended that: (2) (a) The charge for income tax should be based on the profits earned during the period covered by the accounts [p. 10, par. 25].

(b) Where it has been the practice to charge only the minimum or legal liability, then, until full provision has been made for income tax on all profits up to the date of the balance sheet, it is desirable where possible to make provision, in addition, for or towards the balance of the liability for the current and following fiscal years [p. 10, par. 26].

(d) Income tax on revenue taxed before receipt should be included as part of the taxation charge for the year and the relative income should be brought to credit gross [p. 10, par. 28].

(5) Any provision for (or in excess of) the estimated future liability to income tax in respect of the fiscal year commencing after the date of the balance sheet should not be included with current liabilities but should be grouped with reserves or separately stated as a deferred liability and suitably described [p. 10, par. 31].

In the social accounting presentation here put forward provision for direct taxation follows the treatment ordinarily adopted in private accounts by inclusion in the non-operating section of the aggregated profit-and-loss account. It will be noticed that all forms of direct taxation to which business enterprise is subjected are brought together under this heading. Thus in the case of income tax we have the tax on profits, the tax on the ownership of property and the tax on the receivable item of interest and dividends. It may be observed that the income tax which is required to be deducted from the dividends included among the payables in the appropriation account is treated as a set off by way of recovery. Income tax on profits is that assessable for the current accounting period, and which for practical purposes may very well be related to the tax payable in and for the fiscal year in which the close of the accounting period falls. It will be recognised that this question is intimately bound up with the discussion of uniform accounting periods in Section I. Provision for the income tax on profits *assessable* for the current accounting period will have been made in the previous period if we assume that the accounting recommendations we have cited are followed. This is so by reason of the preceding year basis of assessment. Accordingly this provision is brought back as a deduction from the amount actually payable and assessable in the current accounting period, thereby throwing up any over or under provision and a new provision is added for income tax on the *profits of the current accounting period* assessable in the future period. This new provision also appears in the sector balance sheets as a deferred liability at the close of the current accounting period.

When it comes to taxes on excess profits there is no preceding year complication in regard to the basis of assessment so far as concerns the amount payable. On actual payment of the liability it may be found that there was an under or over provision in the previous period which will fall to be adjusted in this the current period. From the standpoint of social accounting it is sought to raise a payable which is related to enterprise income and which will correspond with the receivable in the revenue account of public collective providers.

It will be remarked that we have so far tended to assume that the accounts we are considering are directly institutional in that they relate to corporate enterprise. If we consider the accounts of independent or sole traders, and partnerships we have to recognise that direct taxation is more often than not treated as a personal withdrawal of the person or persons carrying on the enterprise, although in the case of a partnership it is the firm which is assessed. There is also the question of personal allowances which in these cases is commonly set off against the proportionate shares of the statutory measure of operating income. If it were possible we should wish the accounting review of all business enterprises to be treated from the one institutional background in order to preserve a sector view of the matter, and we should like to see direct taxation provisions brought on to the accounts of sole traders and partnerships much in the way we have indicated for corporate enterprises. Apart from the question of personal allowances, it does not seem that there should be any particular difficulty in the case of sole traders, but when it comes to partnerships private accounting must require a prior division of profits to the partners according to their profit-sharing ratios with a subsequent division of the firm's direct liability in terms of the actual liability of each partner, since this division is a personal affair. In these circumstances it is at least convenient to reorganise the direct tax payables of partners as personal matters to be carried into the revenue account of persons in Sector IV—Final Consumers, but this should not be allowed to preclude provisions for deferred liabilities if direct taxation is to be kept in line with the current earnings of continuing business enterprise. On the other hand, since it is aggregated figures with which we are dealing, it would not seem impossible to make the correct allocation to individual partners both of income and direct tax liability, but to draw primary accounts for social purposes on the lines we have indicated. It would then be left to private accounting to identify individual partners' shares of income, direct tax liabilities, withdrawals, and savings retained in the institutional enterprise. It is only right to point out that existing social accounting conventions do not take this view of enterprises conducted by sole traders and partnerships, so that for the present the businesses incomes of such persons are treated as wholly withdrawn for the accounting period, and both taxes and savings are dealt with as personal matters to find their place in Sector IV: Final Consumers—Persons. We should point out, however, that even if sole traders and partnerships are treated as enterprise institutions there are difficulties in the way of carrying the direct tax liabilities attributable to actual withdrawals to the revenue account of persons, a situation which for corporate enterprise is met by the statutory obligation to deduct standard rate income tax at source from the payment of dividends. The formally ideal situation would be a similar treatment for sole trader and partnership withdrawals leaving personal allowances to be identified with the tax attributable to such withdrawals. It seems that in the circumstances this is impracticable and that therefore the present social accounting conventions must stand.

Public Collective Providers—Transfer of Operating Surplus Applicable to Publicly Controlled Enterprises

24 (Originating structure); (2) 26 (Revised structure)

This entry transfers the operating surplus gained from enterprises conducted by public authorities to the Sector (IV) account for public collective providers. It was noted in the originating memorandum on 'A Working System of Social Accounting' that internal sectors may be subdivided into a private and a public authority sphere. The point was made that this was particularly true of productive enterprises and that the distinction was important for a number of reasons. 'The most topical perhaps is the fact that public authority enterprises, being more subject to social control than private enterprises, may be more readily used, through the timing of their capital formation,[1] to help to stabilise the general level of activity. It is therefore important to know the relative contribution made in normal times by these two types of enterprise to domestic capital formation[1] as a whole.' In the accounts here presented this distinction has not been very precisely observed, though we do assume its existence by the transfer of that part of aggregated operating surplus which is attributable to enterprises directed and managed by public collective providers.

Charitable Subscriptions and Donations

24 (Originating structure); (2) 27 (Revised structure)

In the originating structure this item is tacitly treated as a withdrawal. Since, however, it forms a common classification in business accounts it

---

[1] Asset formation.

seems well to make way for it here as a separate debit in the non-operating section of the aggregated profit-and-loss account. It might be observed that such subscriptions as are commonly allowed by the Inland Revenue as expenses for taxation purposes, e.g. a subscription to a local hospital providing a service for the benefit of employees of the enterprise, should be included in the operating section of the account where they will normally fall to be dealt with under the heading for purchases of goods and services as constituting a business subscription specifically related to the earning of revenue.

NET RENTS (BEFORE DEDUCTION OF INCOME TAX) FROM PROPERTY INVESTMENT

(2) 20 (*Revised structure*)

This item has been interpolated in the revised structure set forth here, because it is one which is very often independently noted in business accounts. It will be appreciated that this item will require the construction of an account similar in intention and motive to that contained in the originating structure for Persons (House-ownership). As we have already mentioned elsewhere in this context, where enterprises are engaged in subsidiary economic activities these should be the subject of separate operating accounts.

DIVIDENDS (BEFORE DEDUCTION OF INCOME TAX) AND WITHDRAWALS

(2) 24 (*Originating structure*); (3) 31 (*Revised structure*)

As accountants would expect, this constitutes the main independent item in the appropriation account proper. It should be observed that proposed dividends at the beginning and end of the accounting period are adjusted to actual payments in the manner of creditors in order to reveal the total payables for this classification.

TRANSFER TO RESERVE OF SURPLUS

(2) 29 (*Originating structure*); (3) 32 (*Revised structure*)

This transfer represents retained income and within the existing conventions of social accounting is a measure of corporate enterprise saving. In private accounting parlance it constitutes the increase in the surplus account which, together with contributed capital, forms the main element in the notion of employed capital.

We have already commented under direct taxation on the difficulties occasioned by the distinction in the real world between incorporated and unincorporated enterprise, and since the whole question of business saving is such an important one in the realm of social accounting it seems worth while to reiterate here some pertinent comments which were made by Mr Richard Stone in his originating memorandum, at the same time bearing in mind the reservations in relation to partnerships which were made in the discussion of this subject under the heading of direct taxation. Thus, it was there pointed out that:

In the case of corporate enterprise the distinction between dividend payments and undistributed profit is clear and a distinct meaning can be attached to business saving in this case. With unincorporated enterprise the case is different since here the distinction between the business and personal account of the owner or owners may be much less clear. In the case of partnerships for example the difference is likely to be well defined since the withdrawals are likely to be regulated by agreement and it may be well decided that a part of the income of the period shall not be distributed.[1] In the case of individually owned farms or retail businesses on the other hand, the line will frequently be vague and the distinction between business and personal saving will be arbitrary even when separate business and personal accounts are kept. Accordingly in certain types of unincorporated enterprise it may be best to assume that the whole income is distributed and that any saving done forms part of personal saving. This may not seem satisfactory and is doubtless not a final solution but in handling this problem it is necessary to recognise that the classification of saving recognised by theory into personal and business is blurred in the real world particularly where small scale unincorporated enterprise is the most important type of business organisation.

Nevertheless, for ourselves, we are inclined to the view that if it were not for complicated taxation elements there should be no insuperable bar to the business institutional concept as related to the set-up of accounts both private and social, a concept which would go far to establishing the theoretical distinction between business and personal saving. Professional accountants have long emphasised the vital administrative necessity of maintaining a complete serverance between business and personal accounts, particularly for example in the case of a farmer, a separation which among other things requires the introduction of separate banking accounts, for it will be appreciated that the structure of business account keeping must to some extent be made to rest upon the central record of originating data constituted by the business banking account.

GROSS FIXED ASSET FORMATION

Payments for factors of production—Wages and salaries: 36 (originating structure); (4) 41 (revised structure).

Contributions to social security funds as related to wages and salaries on capital account: (4) 42 (revised structure).

Purchases of goods and services on capital account: 37 (originating structure); (4) 43 (revised structure).

---

[1] But it must not be overlooked that there is a private accounting necessity to make at least a notional distribution of the income earned by the firm during an accounting period, to the partners in their profit-sharing ratios.

Net purchases of existing equipment and other assets on capital account: 38 (originating structure); (4) 45 (revised structure).

Indirect taxes associated with capital transactions, e.g. stamp duties on land: (4) 44 (revised structure).

DEFERRED CHARGES (other than unexpired payments entering into the assessment of circulating capital): (4) 48 (revised structure).

It should be noted that the capital items which together go to make up gross fixed asset formation[1] are still dealt with on a 'payables' basis, and may therefore give rise to opening and closing creditors or accruals. The expression *gross* fixed asset formation is intended to show that some part of the asset formation of the accounting period is not necessarily financed either by borrowing, the depreciation fund or saving, but may be financed by receivable insurance claims as in the case of replacements following a fire.

The payments to labour represent the wages and salaries of the firm's own employees engaged on new construction and installation work, and the contribution to social security funds appropriate to those payments naturally finds inclusion here. The item for the purchases of goods and services on capital account should not present difficulty providing it is thought of in terms of capital construction and equipment of all kinds, e.g. the materials needed by the firm's own employees in the work of new constructions and installations.

We pass to the item for net purchases of existing equipment and other assets on capital account. Existing equipment which is purchased by one undertaking and sold by another within the sector for business enterprises cancels out in the aggregated accounts of that sector. In point of fact, however, such transactions take place with enterprises and persons in other sectors including the rest of the world. As was explained in Mr Stone's originating memorandum 'it seems likely that in some economic systems there will be considerable sales of assets, e.g. motor cars from enterprises to persons through the medium of the second-hand market. Since these sales appear as a negative item in the capital formation[2] of enterprises but as an item of consumers' expenditure in the accounts of persons, they are reflected in the national accounts as negative capital formation'.[2] It is not difficult to see the problems which present themselves when it comes to a question of building up significant aggregates from actual accounts. In the real world accounts are very largely required as a report of stewardship, as a basis for management policy, as a means of determining withdrawable profits, as a basis for the granting of credit, as a means of information for prospective investors, as a guide to the value of existing investments, as an aid to Government supervision, as a basis for price or rate regulation and as a basis for taxation.[3] Thus, there is invariably some relationship with

[1] Capital formation.
[2] Asset formation.
[3] Cf. G. O. May, *Financial Accounting*, pp. 19–21 (New York, Macmillan, 1943).

third parties, e.g. proprietors, but when it comes to a matter of one's own income and expenditure there is not the pressure of necessity to keep very precise accounts providing one has a reasonably clear idea of his or her ability to keep within the limit set by spendable income, and it is unlikely that reasonably accurate accounts will ever be available except from the few. As a consequence it will always be a matter of considerable difficulty to assess the value of durable goods, such as motor cars, in the ownership of persons, and the calculation of national capital must either ignore this very important element or resort to some measure of estimation of a statistical character.

It will be noticed that in the accompanying social accounting set-up we have followed the normal financial accounting procedure of regarding indirect taxes associated with capital transactions as part of the cost of asset formation. The most common example of this kind of tax is the stamp duty payable on the conveyance of land.

The remaining item of deferred charges other than unexpired operating payments entering into the assessment of circulating capital requires some explanation. It is related to payments for services which are not incurred in connection with current output but for the future benefit of an enterprise. Familiar examples are certain types of advertising expenditure. Financial private accounting practice has ordinarily sought to feature this type of expenditure as a separate balance-sheet classification outside that for fixed assets. The idea behind this treatment is to prevent any misconception whereby a deferred charge may be taken as symbolising something real and tangible in the sense of a physical asset. Nevertheless, for social accounting purposes such expenditure falls to be regarded as a part of asset formation within a prescribed current accounting period for the reason that it does not benefit the operations of that period. Accordingly, deferred charges should be brought into calculation with fixed assets in the assessment of asset formation as related to current saving. A moment's reflection will show that this is so when it is remembered that a significant pointer to some measure of economic instability is occasioned by a sharp increase in inventory formation and by an accumulation of liquid balances, both of which belong to that other group of assets lying outside the delayed cost formations we have been considering.

FINANCIAL TRANSACTIONS

Receipts from subscriptions to new issues, etc.: 43 (originating structure); (4) 37 (revised structure).

New borrowing: (a) banks, (b) other financial intermediaries; 44 (originating structure); (4) 38 (revised structure).

Receipts from redemptions and repayments: 45 (originating structure); (4) 39 (revised structure).

Increase in monetary resources: 50 (originating structure); (4) 50 (revised structure).

Subscriptions to new issues, etc.: 51 (originating structure); (4) 46 (revised structure).

Net purchase of existing securities: 52 (originating structure); (4) 47 (revised structure).

Redemption and repayment of obligations: 53 (originating structure); (4) 49 (revised structure).

These items constitute those transactions of an enterprise which are purely financial in character. Apart from the question of saving and the conservation of circulating resources through the agency of replacement funds the finance coming into a business may take the form of receipts from newly contributed capital, new borrowing either long term or short term, and receipts from redemptions and repayments in respect of previous lending by the enterprise. It will be remembered that earlier discussions have pointed to the practical difficulties associated with theoretical conceptions of personal and business savings, and it may be noticed that in the case of unincorporated enterprise the finance provided by the owners even when tantamount to enterprise saving will require to be brought in here as newly contributed capital just as long as it is thought that the institutional view of unincorporated enterprise cannot be maintained.

The item described as increase in monetary resources is merely the excess of the actual receipts of the accounting period over the actual payments in the strict accounting sense of those terms. If it should be negative this merely implies that actual payments have exceeded actual receipts during the period, and to that extent there has been an encroachment into current resources. It is an item which corresponds to that described as 'net sums deposited with banks and given in return for notes and coin',[1] in the originating structure of accounts. In the system put forward here it is supported by a form of receipts and payments account to show the derivation of the entry in the resting account and sector balance sheet.

The subscriptions to new issues 'relate to the purchase by the given enterprise of the new issues of other entities'. The item net purchase of existing securities represents the money outlay on the purchase of existing securities less the money receivables from any sales. In the originating memorandum it was suggested that commissions and handling charges might be debited to operating account, since they could hardly be regarded as forming part of 'capital formation'. Nevertheless, it is well to be clear that private accounting practice does usually treat such charges as part of the money cost of purchasing securities, and conversely such charges as there may be are deducted from the money proceeds when they are sold. As a purely practical matter it would hardly seem worth while to disturb this practice.

The remaining item for redemptions and repayments relates to money outlays by an enterprise in redemption of its own outstanding obligations in respect of past borrowing.

---

[1] (4) Reserve account 50.

IX

THE SECTOR BALANCE SHEETS

SOCIAL ACCOUNTS

Sector I. Business Enterprises

Make up of Balance Sheet Items at Close of Accounting Period

Current liabilities:

Creditors:

i.	For goods delivered on operating account	4,000
ii.	For goods delivered on capital account	46
		4,046

Accrual provisions:

i.	For services rendered on operating account	470
ii.	For wages and salaries on operating account	75
iii.	For accrued interest on borrowed money	20
		565

Current asset:

Unexpired payments:

i.	Indirect taxes (registration licences, local rates, etc.)	40
ii.	Insurance premiums	6
		46

SOCIAL ACCOUNTS

Sector I. Business Enterprises

Pro forma Balance Sheet (in simple outline) on the Basis of a Complete Aggregation of Individual Enterprise Balance Sheets

Liabilities				Assets				
					Par equivalent	**+Premium −Discount**	**Purchase cost**	
I. Capital and surplus:				I. Fixed asset formation (classified by type of asset):				
1. Money capital and capital reserves:				1. Original cost at beginning of accounting period			× ×	×
(a) At beginning of accounting period	...	× ×		2. Formation during the period			× ×	
(b) Contributions during the period	...	× ×		3. Estimated replacement valuation adjustment			×	Negative
2. Surplus and revenue reserves:				II. Property insurance claims (capital)			...	×
(a) At beginning of accounting period	...	×		III. Investments (classified by sector):				
(b) 1. Surplus for the period (retainable income)	×	×		1. At beginning of accounting period	×	×	×	
2. Closing inventory adjustment	×	×		2. Subscriptions to new issues, etc.	×	×	×	
3. Conventional accounting assessment of surplus	...	× ×		3. Net purchases of existing securities	×	×	×	
II. Long-term borrowing (classified by sectors):				IV. Redemptions and repayments				× (Negative)
1. At beginning of accounting period	...	× ×		V. Current assets (classified by sectors where relevant):				
2. New borrowing	...	× ×		1. Inventories of unused materials, work in progress or process, and unsold goods:				
III. Redemption and repayment of obligations:				(a) At beginning of accounting period		×	×	
1. Money capital	...	Negative		(b) Formation during the period		×	×	
2. Long-term borrowing (classified by sectors)	...	Negative		(c) Adjustment to conform with conventional accounting valuation at close of period		×	×	
IV. Depreciation and replacement fund:				2. Debtors		× (Negative)	×	
1. Accumulated original cost allocations	...	× ×		3. Allowance for bad debts		Negative	×	
2. Replacement adjustments	...	× ×		4. Accrual provisions		...	×	
V. Current liabilities (classified by sectors):				5. Unexpired payments		...	×	
1. Short-term borrowing	...	× ×		6. Bank and cash balances		...	×	
2. Creditors	...	× ×		VI. Deferred charges¹ and other items		...	...	×
3. Accrual provisions	...	× ×						
4. Proposed dividends	...	× ×						
VI. Deferred liabilities	...	...						

¹ Other than unexpired payments entering into the assessment of circulating capital

SOCIAL ACCOUNTS

SECTOR I. BUSINESS ENTERPRISES

BALANCE SHEET AT CLOSE OF ACCOUNTING PERIOD (*Limited to the entries of the period*)

I. Capital and surplus:			
1. Circulating capital fund at beginning of accounting period[1]	...	1,020	
2. Money capital contributions during the period[1]	...	345	
3. (a) Surplus for the period (retainable income equivalent to corporate enterprise saving)	105		
(b) Closing inventory adjustment	5		
(c) Conventional accounting assessment of surplus	...	110	1,475
II. New borrowing:			
1. Banks	...	25	
2. Other financial intermediaries	...	40	65
III. Redemptions and repayment of obligations	...	1,540 −20	1,520
IV. Depreciation and replacement fund:			
1. Arithmetical allocation based on original cost	...	300	
2. Replacement adjustment	...	140	440
V. Current liabilities:			
1. Creditors	...	4,046	
2. Accrual provisions	...	565	4,611
3. Proposed dividends	...	30	4,641
VI. Deferred liability. Income tax on the profits of the current accounting period assessable in the future period	...	...	45
			6,646

I. Gross fixed asset formation:			
1. Payments for factors of production. Wages and salaries and salaries on capital account	...	135	
2. Contributions to social security funds as related to wages	...	...	
3. Purchases of goods and services	...	800	
4. Net purchases of existing equipment and other assets on capital account	...	15	
5. Indirect taxes associated with capital transactions, e.g. stamp duties on land	...	950 −35	915
II. Property insurance claims (Capital)	...	...	
III. Investments:			
1. Subscriptions to new issues, etc.	...	30	
2. Net purchases of existing securities	...	5	35
IV. Redemptions and repayments	...	...	
V. Current assets:			
1. Inventories of unused materials, work in progress or process, and unsold goods:			
(a) At beginning of accounting period	55		
(b) Formation during the period	10		
(c) Adjustment to conform with conventional accounting valuation at close of period	5	950 −15	935
2. Debtors	5,000 −25		
3. Allowance for bad debts	5	70	
4. Unexpired payments	...	4,975 46	
5. Accrual provision for interest	...	2	
6. Net increase in money resources	...	618	5,711
VI. Deferred charges (other than unexpired payments entering into the assessment of circulating capital)	...	...	...
			6,646

[1] Includes subscriptions to new issues.

X

GLOSSARY OF TERMS

Accrued expenses. An amount, usually calculated on a time basis, intended to cover services rendered but not paid for at accounting dates.

Appropriation account. The working account of an enterprise which portrays the amount of available income from all sources applicable to a relevant accounting period, that part of it which is distributed by way of dividends to and withdrawals of proprietors, and that part which is reserved as business saving.

Balancing statement. A summarised list of classified entries in debit and credit columnar form designed to show that all the items entering into a system of accounts are in a state of balance. In accounting terminology this statement is called a 'Trial Balance'.

Capital. In general terms the amount of money contributed to an enterprise by its proprietors to finance the acquisition of fixed and circulating assets.

Circulating capital. The net working resources of an enterprise equivalent to the amount of its current assets minus its short-term liabilities, both currently due for payment and accrued, at accounting dates. These resources are commonly described by accountants as working capital.

Creditor. In this context a monetary liability for goods delivered and services rendered but not paid for at a particular accounting date.

Current assets. Those assets of an enterprise which are normally held for realisation in the ordinary course of business, e.g. inventories, debtors, bank balances and cash. (See *The Recommendations on Accounting Principles of the Institute of Chartered Accountants*, p. 22.)

Debtor. In this context an amount of money owing to an enterprise at a particular accounting date for goods delivered and services rendered.

Deferred charge. A payment for a service which is not incurred in connection with current output but for the future benefit of an enterprise.

Depreciation and Obsolescence. In this context an amount provided out of the operating receivables of an enterprise to build up a fund which will conserve circulating resources sufficient to enable equipment to be replaced by the time it is worn out or obsolete.

Fixed asset formation. The expenditure in a given accounting period incurred on equipment and such like capital assets held with the object of earning revenue and not for the purpose of sale in the ordinary course of business. (See *Recommendations on Accounting Principles of the Institute of Chartered Accountants*, p. 24 (i).)

Inventory formation. The *real* increase in unused materials, work in progress, and unsold goods as between two accounting dates, sought to be measured statistically by the accounting device of pegging the pricing of the closing inventory in terms of the opening inventory.

Investment. The expenditure in a given accounting period incurred on subscriptions to new issues and the purchase of existing securities.

Payables. Amounts of money due and assignable in respect of the obligations of, the goods delivered and services rendered to, an enterprise, institution or person, during a given period of account.

Payment. A sum of money actually paid in terms of cash.

Private accounting. The accounting of the individual firm. (See Hicks, *The Social Framework*, p. vi.)

Receipt. A sum of money actually received in terms of cash.

Receivables. Amounts of money due and assignable in respect of obligations to, goods delivered and services rendered by, an enterprise, institution or person during a given period of account.

Reserve. An amount of available income or other gain saved by an enterprise.

Resting account. The account which shows the sources which finance asset formation and investment purchases during a given period of account. The term resting is used for this account to distinguish it from the profit-and-loss account of the active working of an enterprise.

Social accounting. The accounting of the whole community or nation. (See Hicks, *The Social Framework*, p. vi.)

Unexpired payment. That part of an operating payment the benefit for which will arise in the immediate future.

APPENDIX I. A FURTHER NOTE ON PROVISIONS FOR DEPRECIATION AND OBSOLESCENCE

In Section VIII of this book we have sought to explain the operating debit for depreciation and obsolescence in the accounts of business enterprises and we have been at pains to underline the contention that the economic concept of such provision requires the building up of funds which will so point to the conservation of resources as to enable items of fixed equipment to be readily replaced, without recourse to new borrowing, by the time they are worn out or obsolete. The measurement of these replacement funds involves the consideration of at least two issues.

The first is associated with the economic dimension of operating surplus and is thereby concerned with the temporal allocations attributable to current operations. We have seen that conventional accounting measures these allocations by reference to the original costs of fixed assets, as related to time periods of effective user. A strict application of this method requires that each asset should be treated separately, which means that the accounting provision which finds its way to the debit of profit-and-loss account is constituted by a summation of the allocations as arithmetically calculated for individual assets. For the economic purposes of social accounts we need to reset this provision for charge to operating account in terms of current replacement costs. This too will mean a resetting for each individual asset. The total of such replacement cost allocations attributable to the relevant accounting period will constitute the economic provision for depreciation and obsolescence to be included with the payables in the operating section of the profit-and-loss account.

The second issue gives rise to problems which are concerned with adjustments intended to cover the inadequacy or otherwise of accumulating replacement fund totals when judged in the light of replacement costs at the close of the particular accounting period under survey. It is plain that while the current economic provision is a sufficient replacement carry for attribution to the operating account of the current accounting period, the store of back provisions accumulating in the fund may be out of line unless brought up to date by some adjusting reservation.

If we turn to the *pro forma* balance sheet at Section IX of this book as set up on the basis of a complete aggregation of individual enterprise balance sheets we shall see that the control of fixed asset formation at original money cost involves a passive inset carry for the estimated replacement valuation adjustment in order that, by abstraction, such part of the national capital may be taken in at its current replacement cost after setting off the depreciation and replacement fund on a like basis. If this gross revaluation adjustment is brought on to the balance sheet as an active entry, then it must promote another counterbalancing entry in a capital reserve or capital surplus account. Thereafter, a transfer out of this particular account will be required in order to cover the back adjustments to the replacement fund, leaving a balance which is equivalent to the change in the residual book values of the fixed assets (i.e. as related to their unexpired original cost values) plus such replacement provisions, in excess of original cost allocations, as have been found out of operating account. Thus if prices have risen the residual book values of the fixed assets on hand will have increased, and this appreciation is part of the positive balance which will remain in the capital reserve or surplus account as a result of the technical accounting procedure we have indicated.

The depreciation fund as set to include the back adjustments may be said to give the maximum position for the conservation of replacement resources. On the assumption of realisable residual asset replacement values and appropriate availability of replacement resources it would mean that the whole of the fixed equipment of an enterprise could be replaced at one time. In the ordinary run of business affairs it is quite unlikely that an individual firm will ever find itself in the position of having to renew the whole of its fixed equipment at the one time. On the other hand if it is efficiently managed it will have a reasonably close idea of the extent of its real capital commitments in the oncoming period of account. The estimated measurement of such commitments on a replacement basis should therefore mark the point of immediate conservation of circulating resources over and above those required to finance the current working of the enterprise. On the other hand if it became apparent that an even tenor of asset formation was unlikely because in fact preponderating replacements *were* maturing at the one time, or because of a high obsolescence factor generating over a disproportionate part of the fixed equipment, then it might be necessary to cover any immediate investment inadequacy of accumulated back provisions, due to price change and investment in monetary claims, by a present profit retention in excess of the current economic provision for depreciation and obsolescence. Such a special provision would find its way to the non-operating section of the profit-and-loss account to end up as a part of capital reserve or capital surplus account. In the circumstances we have considered, the necessity for this special provision would have become apparent and in the context of the social accounts, as set down in Section VII of this book, might well be found out of the non-operating credit for capital gains, by appropriate negative entry.

From what has been said it will be detected that there may be occasions when some degree of correlation can be established between the periodic replacement provision and the periodic replacement commitments, a correlation which in part requires that actual replacements are evenly spread. As we have observed, it is then only necessary to safeguard the circulating resources of the replacement fund in equivalence with the replacement commitments. The maintenance of real capital intact implies the *real* preservation of replacement funds. In so far as such funds are represented by money claims they will suffer depreciation in a period of rising prices, a situation which should be made good out of current account in the way we have indicated. This requires some watchfulness on the part of business managements and is best safeguarded by reducing replacement fund investments in money claims to a minimum consistent with replacement commitments.

APPENDIX II. A FURTHER NOTE ON INVENTORIES

In Section VIII of this book we hinted at the problems associated with the maintenance of inventories and in this connection it is convenient to consider the maintenance of total inventories. Suppose in the first instance that inventories expressed in quantities are increased over the period of account. Then in order to see the effect of this inventory change on the measurement of profit it would be virtually necessary to value the quantitative increase at or near to last cost. As a consequence of this procedure the closing credit for inventory valuation in the operating account would be equivalent to the amount of the opening debit plus the quantitative increase at last cost.

If we suppose in the second instance that inventories expressed in quantities have decreased over the period of account, then since there is *no* quantitative increase there will be *no* addition to value at last cost, and the whole of the closing inventory will remain valued at what we may call the first cost represented by the basis of valuation of the opening inventory. In this case, however, since there has been a fall in quantities it may be necessary to provide for an operating item which takes care of the difference between the first or opening and last or closing costs on the quantitative decrease. The purpose of this adjustment is to safeguard the financial ability of the enterprise to restore the quantitative amount of its opening inventory. When this restoration is carried out the replacement provision then standing in the balance sheet will fall to be dealt with as a capital surplus adjustment. Although there may appear to be an asymmetry of treatment between the methods adopted in the two situations it will really be seen that each method has *the same net effect* on the operating account, and is equivalent to controlling opening and closing inventories at last cost so far as this net effect is concerned. In either case the difference between the closing and the opening inventories plus or minus the operating entry introduced in the case of falling inventories, is equivalent to the change in the quantities valued at last cost. This net effect is sometimes referred to as inventory formation valued at last cost. In the context of this discussion it is convenient, as a matter of accounting mechanics, to adjust the *total* closing inventory to a *balance-sheet* valuation at last or replacement cost thereby giving rise to a capital surplus adjustment equivalent to the difference between the first or opening and the last or replacement cost, of the quantitative amount of the opening inventory in the case of a positive formation, or the quantitative amount of the closing inventory in the case of a negative formation. This *total* last or replacement cost *balance-sheet* valuation of the closing inventory will then stand as the operating account valuation of the opening inventory of the succeeding period.

We have considered the maintenance of total inventories because the methods enunciated show the essential principles involved. For the individual enterprise there may be a further problem, to be regarded as a development of this approach, whereby the maintenance of inventories is limited to the *normal* quantitative carry appropriate to the scale of output of that particular enterprise. It will be seen that this is a view of the matter which is closely akin to the accounting conception of a base stock.

As a final comment, we would remark that in order to safeguard the stability of an individual enterprise, that part of its working capital which in a period of rising prices is represented by depreciating monetary claims, may be restored to its value in real terms by an appropriate debit provision, to cover the depreciation, in the non-operating section of the profit-and-loss account. Such provision will then fall to be credited to capital reserve or surplus account.

APPENDIX III. SOCIAL ACCOUNTING

SUGGESTED FORM OF BUSINESS ENTERPRISE PRIMARY ACCOUNTING RETURN[1]—PROFIT-AND-LOSS ACCOUNT

OPERATING SECTION

	Payables	£	£	£
A. PRODUCTION:				
I. Inventories at beginning of accounting period:				
	1. Raw materials	×		
	2. Consumable tools and/or sundry stores	×		
	3. Work in progress or process	×		
		×		
II. Inventories at close of accounting period:				
	1. Raw materials	×		
	2. Consumable tools and/or sundry stores	×		
	3. Work in progress or process	×		
		×		
III. Increase (−) or decrease (+) in inventories:				
	1. Raw materials	×		
	2. Consumable tools and/or sundry stores	×		
	3. Work in progress or process	×		
			×	
IV. Inventory replacement provisions:				
	(+ or −)	...	×	
V. Purchases of goods and services:				
	1. Raw materials	×		
	2. Consumable tools and/or sundry stores	×		
	3. Intermediate goods (e.g. bought out parts) and/or sub-contract work	×		
	4. Carriage inwards	×		
	5. Rent of factory	×		
	6. Fuel and power	×		
	7. Factory lighting, heating and water	×		
	8. Repairs and maintenance of factory buildings[2]	×		
	9. Repairs and maintenance of plant and machinery[2]	×		
	10. Royalties and machine rents	×		
	11. Servicing of lifts and runways[2]	×		
	12. Servicing of transport equipment[2]	×		
	13. Works printing, telephones, telegrams, travelling and such like items	×		
	14. Miscellaneous works expenses	×		
		×		
	15. Less discounts received	×		
			×	

Proportional or variable	×
Semi-fixed or semi-variable	×
Fixed or standing	×
	×

Forward   ×

[1] The detailed classifications noted in this return are only intended as a guide to accountants. They are put forward as representing the most likely classifications which a number of companies would have in their financial ledgers. It is the major groupings which are important because they fall into line with the social accounting structure discussed in this book.

[2] These classifications should *not* include any wages of the employees of the enterprise, as such payables should appear under the primary heading for Wages.

		£	£	£
Payables				
Brought forward			×	

VI. Indirect taxes:
    1. Excise duty   ×
    2. Factory rates   ×
    3. Transport registration dues   ×
                                                ×

VII. Wages and salaries:
    1. Direct wages to operatives (including bonuses and holiday pay)   ×
    2. Wages of foremen and supervisors   ×
    3. Motor-drivers' wages   ×
    4. Salaries of works managers, technical directors and their assistants   ×
                       ×

VIII. Contributions to social security funds:
    1. State insurances   ×
    2. Private pension funds   ×
            ×   ×

Proportional or variable	×
Semi-fixed or semi-variable	×
Fixed or standing	×
	×

IX. (i) Depreciation and obsolescence (original costs):
    1. Factory buildings   ×
    2. Plant and machinery   ×
    3. Transport equipment   ×
         ×

  (ii) Additional replacement provisions (+ or −) (suitably detailed)   ×   ×

X. Factory insurances: ×   ×

B. SELLING AND DISTRIBUTION:
  I. Inventory of finished goods at beginning of accounting period   ×

  II. Inventory of finished goods at close of accounting period   ×

  III. Increase (−) or decrease (+) in inventory of finished goods   ...   ×
  IV. Inventory replacement provision (+ or −)   ...   ×
  V. Purchases of goods and services:
    1. Rent of warehouses, salesrooms, etc.   ×
    2. Advertising, exhibitions, catalogues, etc.   ×
    3. Lighting, heating and water applicable to warehouses and salesrooms   ×
    4. Repairs and maintenance of warehouse and salesroom buildings[1]   ×
    5. Repairs and maintenance of warehouse and salesroom equipment[1]   ×
    6. Servicing of warehouse and salesroom lifts and runways[1]   ×
    7. Servicing of transport equipment[1]   ×
    8. Printing, telephones, telegrams and such like items   ×
    9. Travelling and entertaining expenses of salesmen, sales directors and their assistants   ×
    10. Miscellaneous selling expenses   ×
                ×

Forward   ×   ×   ×

[1] These classifications should *not* include any wages of the employees of the enterprise, as such payables should appear under the primary heading for Wages.

Payables

	£	£	£
Brought forward	×	×	×
11. Less discounts received	×		
		×	

Proportional or variable	×
Semi-fixed or semi-variable	×
Fixed or standing	×
	×

VI. Indirect taxes:

	£	£
1. Purchase tax	×	
2. Rates of warehouses, salesrooms, etc.	×	
3. Transport registration dues	×	
		×

Proportional or variable	×
Fixed or standing	×
	×

VII. Wages and salaries:

	£
1. Wages of warehousemen and salesroom assistants (including bonuses and holiday pay)	×
2. Wages of supervisors	×
3. Motor-drivers' wages	×
4. Salaries of salesmen, sales directors and their assistants	×
5. Salesmen's commissions	×
	×

VIII. Contributions to social security funds:

	£	£	£
1. State insurances	×		
2. Private pension funds	×		
		×	
			×

Proportional or variable	×
Semi-fixed or semi-variable	×
Fixed or standing	×
	×

IX. (i) Depreciation and obsolescence (original costs):

	£	£	£
1. Warehouse and salesroom buildings	×		
2. Warehouse and salesroom equipment	×		
3. Transport equipment	×		
		×	
(ii) Additional replacement provisions (+ or −) (suitably detailed)		×	
			×
X. Warehouse and salesroom insurances	...		×
XI. Bad debts and debt collection expenses	...		×
			×
Forward			×

	£	£	£
Payables			
Brought forward			×
C. ADMINISTRATION AND MANAGEMENT:			
I. Purchases of goods and services:			
1. Rent of offices, etc.	×		
2. Office lighting, heating and water	×		
3. Office cleaning[1]	×		
4. Repairs and maintenance of office buildings[1]	×		
5. Repairs and maintenance of office equipment[1]	×		
6. Servicing of office lifts[1]	×		
7. Printing and stationery	×		
8. Postages, telephones, telegrams and such like items	×		
9. Travelling and other expenses of administrative directors and their assistants	×		
10. Trade subscriptions	×		
11. Professional charges	×		
12. Miscellaneous office expenses	×		
	×		
13. Less discounts received (if any)	×		
		×	
Semi-fixed or semi-variable	×		
Fixed or standing	×		
	×		
II. Banks and other financial intermediaries:			
Commission charges for keeping accounts and other services	...	×	
III. Indirect taxes:			
Rates of offices, etc.	...	×	
IV. Salaries and fees:			
1. Salaries of office staff	×		
2. Remuneration of administrative directors	×		
	×		
V. Contributions to social security funds:			
1. State insurances ×	×		
2. Private pension funds ×	×		
		×	
Semi-fixed or semi-variable	×		
Fixed or standing	×		
	×		
VI. (i) Depreciation and obsolescence (original costs):			
1. Office buildings ×			
2. Office equipment (including furniture and fixtures) ×	×		
(ii) Additional replacement provisions (+ or −) (suitably detailed)	×		
		×	
VII. Insurances	...	×	
			×
D. INTEREST ON BORROWED MONEY (before deduction of income tax)	...	...	×
Total payables			×
E. OPERATING SURPLUS	...	...	×
Total debits			×

[1] These classifications should *not* include any wages of the employees of the enterprise, as such payables should appear under the primary heading for Wages.

Receivables

	£	£
I. Net sales[1] of goods and services	×	
Less discounts allowed	×	
		×
II. Subsidies	...	×
Total receivables and credits		×

[1] I.e. after deduction of all returns and allowances other than cash discounts.

PROFIT-AND-LOSS ACCOUNT

Non-Operating Section

Payables

	£	£	£	£
I. Direct taxation:				
Direct taxes assessable for the current accounting period				
1. Income tax on profit ×				
2. Income tax on the ownership of property ×				
3. Income tax on interest and dividends ×				
×				
4. *Less* Income tax recovered from the dividends included among the payables in the appropriation account ×				
	×			
5. Profits tax	×			
		×		
Deduct:				
6. Income tax on profits assessable for the current accounting period as provided in the previous period	×			
7. Profits tax over provided in the previous period	×			
		×		
			×	
8. Income tax on the profits of the current accounting period assessable in the future period	...	...	×	
				×
II. Contingency claims to employees and third parties	...	...	...	×
III. Charitable subscriptions and donations	...	...	...	×
Total payables				×
IV. Transfer to appropriation account of surplus	...	...	...	×
Total debits				×

Receivables

	£
I. Operating surplus	×
II. Interest and dividends (before deduction of income tax)	×
III. Net rents from property investments (before deduction of income tax)	×
IV. Net realised capital gains: available for distribution as income	×
V. Insurance claims in respect of consequential loss and contingency claims to employees and third parties	×
Total receivables and credits	×

APPROPRIATION ACCOUNT

	£
I. Dividends (before deduction of income tax) and withdrawals	×
II. Retained surplus	×
III. Surplus from non-operating section	×

RESTING ACCOUNT (BALANCE-SHEET MOVEMENTS)

	£	£
I. Gross fixed asset formation:		
1. Wages and salaries	×	
2. State insurance	×	
3. Purchases of goods and services	×	
4. Indirect taxes associated with capital transactions, e.g. stamp duties on land	×	
5. Net purchases of existing equipment and other assets on capital account	×	
		×
II. Investments:		
1. Subscriptions to new issues, etc.	×	
2. Net purchases of existing securities (adjusted for transfers of profits or losses on realisations[1])	×	
		×
III. Movements in deferred charges (other than unexpired payments entering into the assessment of circulating capital)	...	×
IV. Payments for redemptions and repayment of obligations	...	×
V. Movements in circulating capital funds:		
1. Closing inventories	×	
2. *Less* opening inventories	×	
3. Inventory formation	...	×
4. Closing net debtors[2]	×	
5. *Less* opening net debtors	×	
		×
6. Closing money resources	×	
7. *Less* opening money resources	×	
		×
Total debits		×

[1] The net total of these transfers should be separately detailed as an inset adjustment.
[2] I.e. Debtors less creditors.

	£	£
I. Depreciation and obsolescence and additional replacement provisions	...	×
II. Inventory replacement provisions	...	×
III. Property insurance claims received (capital)	...	×
IV. Appropriation account (retained surplus)	...	×
V. Net money capital contributions	...	×
VI. New borrowing	...	×
VII. Receipts from redemptions and repayments	...	×
VIII. Movements in deferred liabilities:		
1. Closing deferred liability—income tax on the profits of the current accounting period assessable in the future period	×	
2. *Less* opening deferred liability—income tax	×	
		×
Total credits		×

BALANCE SHEET: ASSETS

	£	£	£
I. Fixed assets (classified by type of asset):			
1. Original cost at beginning of accounting period	...	×	
2. Formation during the period	×		
Less property insurance claims received	×		
		×	
		×	
3. Estimated replacement valuation adjustment	...	×	
			×
II. Investments:			

	Par equivalent	+ Premium − Discount	Purchase cost	
1. At beginning of accounting period	×	×	×	
2. Subscriptions to new issues, etc.	×	×	×	
3. Net purchases of existing securities (adjusted for transfers of profits or losses on realisations)	×	×	×	
4. Redemptions and repayments (negative)	×	×	×	×
	×	×	×	

	£	£	£
III. Current assets:			
1. Inventories (suitably detailed):			
(a) At beginning of accounting period	×		
(b) Formation during the period	×		
	×		
(c) Replacement valuation adjustment	×		
		×	
2. Debtors	...	×	
3. Accrual provisions	...	×	
4. Unexpired payments	...	×	
5. Bank and cash balances	...	×	
			×
IV. Deferred charges and other items (suitably detailed)	...	...	×
			×

BALANCE SHEET: CAPITAL AND LIABILITIES

	£	£	£
I. Capital and surplus:			
1. Money capital (suitably detailed):			
(a) At beginning of accounting period	×		
(b) Contributions during the period (less redemptions and repayments)	×		
		×	
2. Capital reserves or surplus:			
(a) At beginning of accounting period	×		
(b) Adjustments during the period	×		
		×	
3. Revenue reserves or surplus			
(a) At beginning of accounting period	×		
(b) Retained surplus of the period	×		
		×	
			×
II. Long-term borrowing:			
1. At beginning of accounting period	...	×	
2. New borrowing (less redemptions and repayments)	...	×	
			×
III. Depreciation fund:			
1. Accumulated original cost allocations	...	×	
2. Additional replacement provisions:			
(a) Operating account	×		
(b) Capital reserve	×		
		×	
			×
IV. Inventory replacement provisions	...	...	×
V. Current liabilities:			
1. Short-term borrowing	...	×	
2. Creditors	...	×	
3. Accrual provisions	...	×	
		×	
4. Proposed dividends	...	×	
			×
VI. Deferred liabilities	...	...	×
			×